Creative Cooking

AN AMERICAN TRADITION

VELVEETA Pasteurized Process Cheese Spread has been served in American homes for more than a half a century and can be considered truly a "slice of Americana." Millions of Americans have warm childhood memories that include their favorite recipe made with VELVEETA Process Cheese Spread.

Today, VELVEETA Process Cheese Spread is still America's favorite cooking cheese because of its flavor, cooking versatility and ease of use. Since most households now have two members working, more time is being spent at leisure activities and less is being devoted to household chores and cooking. These busy lifestyles call for quick and simple recipes that are pleasing to the eye, easy to prepare and nutritious. VELVEETA Process Cheese Spread, with its smooth creamy melt, performs culinary magic in everything from tasty snacks and appetizers to sumptuous entrees and vegetable dishes.

VELVEETA Process Cheese Spread, the product that millions of Americans have grown up with, is today's time-tested answer to fast, fresh, imaginative and delicious meals.

■ *NEW AMERICAN FAVORITES*

VELVEETA Pasteurized Process Cheese Spread is a product with a heritage of cooking versatility and ease of use, and these qualities are more important than ever to today's busy cooks. To bring even more convenience into the kitchen, that delicious blend of natural cheeses found in VELVEETA Process Cheese Spread is now available in other easy-to-use forms and flavors.

The VELVEETA Mexican varieties, both Mild and Hot, provide a touch of zesty jalapeño pepper for those occasions when you want to put a little "south-of-the-border" accent into your cooking. VELVEETA Shredded Process Cheese Food is the newest addition to the VELVEETA family of products. Available in Original, and Mild and Hot Mexican varieties, it has a creamy flavor that enhances your recipes in ways other shredded cheeses can't. You'll find these newer forms and flavors of VELVEETA products particularly suited for many of the recipes found in this magazine.

All VELVEETA products are ideal for either traditional or microwave cooking, and you'll find microwaving instructions included for most of these outstanding recipes. From a simple sandwich to cheesy pasta dishes to savory sauces, VELVEETA products help you create fresh, attractive meals with ease and style. It's the way to go for today's fast-paced cook-on-the-go.

SNACKS

■ HOT BROCCOLI DIP

6 to 8 servings

1 1½-lb. round sourdough bread loaf
½ cup finely chopped celery
½ cup chopped red pepper
¼ cup finely chopped onion
2 tablespoons PARKAY Margarine
1 lb. VELVEETA Pasteurized Process Cheese Spread, cubed
1 10-oz. pkg. frozen chopped broccoli, thawed, drained
¼ teaspoon dried rosemary leaves, crushed

Cut slice from top of bread loaf; remove center leaving 1-inch shell. Cut removed bread into bite-size pieces. Cover shell with top. Place on cookie sheet with bread pieces. Bake at 350°, 15 minutes or until hot. In large skillet, saute celery, peppers and onions in margarine. Reduce heat to low. Add process cheese spread; stir until melted. Stir in remaining ingredients; heat thoroughly, stirring constantly. Spoon into bread loaf. Serve hot with toasted bread pieces and vegetable dippers.

Preparation time: 15 minutes
Baking time: 15 minutes

Microwave: Prepare bread loaf as directed. Combine celery, peppers, onions and margarine in 2-quart microwave-safe bowl. Microwave on High 1 minute. Add remaining ingredients; microwave on High 5 to 6 minutes or until hot, stirring after 3 minutes. Spoon into bread loaf. Serve hot with toasted bread pieces and vegetable dippers.

Hot Broccoli Dip

SAUCY SPANISH MEATBALLS

Approximately 5 dozen

1½ lbs. ground beef
½ cup dry bread crumbs
½ cup milk
1 egg, beaten
⅛ teaspoon ground cumin
Dash of pepper
                    *   *   *
½ cup chopped onion
2 tablespoons PARKAY
   Margarine
1 lb. VELVEETA Mexican
   Pasteurized Process Cheese
   Spread with Jalapeño
   Pepper, cubed
1 14½-oz. can tomatoes,
   chopped, drained
¼ teaspoon ground cumin

In large bowl, combine meat, crumbs, milk, egg and seasonings; mix lightly. Shape into 1-inch meatballs. Bake at 400°, 20 minutes, turning occasionally.

Saute onions in margarine. Reduce heat to low. Add remaining ingredients; stir until process cheese spread is melted. Serve with meatball dippers.

Preparation time: 20 minutes
Baking time: 20 minutes

Microwave: Prepare meatballs as directed. Microwave onions and margarine in 1½-quart microwave-safe bowl on High 1 minute. Add remaining ingredients. Microwave on High 7 to 8 minutes or until thoroughly heated, stirring after 4 minutes. Serve with meatball dippers.

Buenos Nachos

PEPPY SPREAD

2½ cups

2 cups (8 ozs.) VELVEETA
   Mexican Shredded
   Pasteurized Process Cheese
   Food with Jalapeño Pepper
1 8-oz. pkg. PHILADELPHIA
   BRAND Cream Cheese,
   softened
1 4¼-oz. can deviled ham
2 tablespoons chopped green
   onion
2 tablespoons milk
½ teaspoon Worcestershire
   sauce

Combine process cheese food and cream cheese, mixing at medium speed on electric mixer until well blended. Stir in remaining ingredients. Cover; chill. Serve with assorted crackers.

Preparation time: 5 minutes plus
chilling

■ BUENOS NACHOS

6 to 8 servings

    1 8-oz. pkg. PHILADELPHIA
        BRAND Cream Cheese,
        softened
    ¾ cup guacamole
    ½ cup sour cream
        Tortilla chips
    ½ lb. VELVEETA Mexican
        Pasteurized Process Cheese
        Spread with Jalapeño
        Pepper, cubed
    3 tablespoons milk
    ½ cup chopped tomato
    ¼ cup pitted ripe olive slices
    2 tablespoons green onion
        slices

Combine cream cheese, guacamole and sour cream, mixing until well blended. Spread cream cheese mixture onto serving platter; top with chips. Combine process cheese spread and milk in saucepan; stir over low heat until process cheese spread is melted. Cover chips with process cheese spread mixture; top with remaining ingredients.

Preparation time: 10 minutes
Cooking time: 5 minutes

Florentine Crescents

■ FLORENTINE CRESCENTS

32 appetizers

- 1 10-oz. pkg. frozen chopped spinach, thawed, well-drained
- ½ lb. VELVEETA Pasteurized Process Cheese Spread, cubed
- ¼ cup dry bread crumbs
- 3 crisply cooked bacon slices, crumbled
- 2 8-oz. cans PILLSBURY Refrigerated Quick Crescent Dinner Rolls

In 2-quart saucepan, combine spinach, process cheese spread, crumbs and bacon. Stir over low heat until process cheese spread is melted. Unroll dough; separate into sixteen triangles. Cut each in half lengthwise, forming thirty-two triangles. Spread each triangle with rounded teaspoonful spinach mixture. Roll up, starting at wide end. Place on greased cookie sheet. Brush dough with beaten egg, if desired. Bake at 375°, 11 to 13 minutes or until golden brown.

Preparation time: 20 minutes
Baking time: 13 minutes per batch.

Microwave: Combine spinach, process cheese spread, crumbs and bacon in 1½-quart microwave-safe bowl. Microwave on High 2½ to 4½ minutes or until process cheese spread is melted, stirring every 1½ minutes. Continue as directed.

■ MEXICAN CORN BREAD

4 to 6 servings

¼ lb. VELVEETA Mexican
    Pasteurized Process Cheese
    Spread with Jalapeño
    Pepper, cubed
2 tablespoons milk
1 egg, beaten
1 8½-oz. pkg. corn muffin mix

Combine process cheese spread and
milk in saucepan; stir over low heat
until process cheese spread is melted. Add process cheese spread mixture and egg to muffin mix, mixing
just until moistened. Pour into
greased 8-inch square pan. Bake at
350°, 20 minutes.

Preparation time: 10 minutes
Baking time: 20 minutes

Variation: Substitute VELVEETA Pas-
teurized Process Cheese Spread for
Process Cheese Spread with Jalapeño
Pepper.

■ CREAMY CLAM DIP

6 to 8 servings

1 8-oz. pkg. PHILADELPHIA
    BRAND Cream Cheese,
    softened
¼ lb. VELVEETA Pasteurized
    Process Cheese Spread,
    cubed
2 tablespoons milk
1 6½-oz. can minced clams,
    drained
2 tablespoons green onion
    slices
⅛ teaspoon dill weed

Combine cream cheese, process
cheese spread and milk, mixing at
medium speed on electric mixer until well blended. Stir in remaining ingredients. Spoon into 9-inch pie plate.
Bake at 350°, 15 to 18 minutes or
until lightly browned. Serve with
crackers, chips or vegetable dippers.

Preparation time: 5 minutes
Baking time: 18 minutes

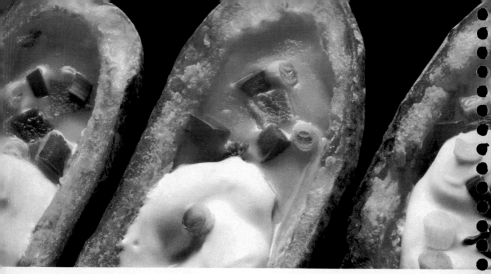

Cheesy Potato Skins

■ CHEESY POTATO SKINS

8 appetizers

**4 large baking potatoes, baked
   Oil
¼ lb. VELVEETA Pasteurized
   Process Cheese Spread,
   cubed
2 tablespoons chopped red or
   green pepper
2 crisply cooked bacon slices,
   crumbled
1 tablespoon green onion slices
   Sour cream**

Cut potatoes in half lengthwise; scoop out centers, leaving ¼-inch shell. Fry shells, a few at a time, in deep hot oil, 375°, 2 to 3 minutes or until golden brown; drain. Place on cookie sheet. Top with process cheese spread; broil until process cheese spread begins to melt. Top with remaining ingredients.

*Preparation time: 60 minutes
Cooking time: 10 minutes*

■ BEAN DIP OLÉ

4 cups

**1 lb. VELVEETA Pasteurized
   Process Cheese Spread,
   cubed
1 16-oz. can refried beans
1 4-oz. can chopped green
   chilies
¼ cup milk**

In 2-quart saucepan, combine ingredients; stir over low heat until process cheese spread is melted. Serve hot with tortilla chips.

*Preparation time: 5 minutes
Cooking time: 10 minutes*

Variation: Substitute VELVEETA Mexican Pasteurized Process Cheese Spread with Jalapeño Pepper for Process Cheese Spread.

Microwave: Combine ingredients in 2-quart microwave-safe bowl. Microwave on High 8 to 9 minutes or until thoroughly heated, stirring every 4 minutes. Serve hot with tortilla chips.

NACHOS DE POLLO

6 to 8 servings

¾ **lb. VELVEETA Mexican**
    Pasteurized Process Cheese
    Spread with Jalapeño
    Pepper, cubed
1 **cup chopped cooked chicken**
½ **cup chopped onion**
½ **cup chopped green pepper**
¼ **cup milk**
    Tortilla chips
1 **cup chopped tomato**

In 2-quart saucepan, combine process cheese spread, chicken, onions, peppers and milk; stir over low heat until process cheese spread is melted. Cover serving platter with chips; top with chicken mixture and tomatoes.

Preparation time: 10 minutes
Cooking time: 10 minutes

Variation: Place 2 cups shredded lettuce over chicken mixture; top with tomatoes.

Microwave: Combine process cheese spread, chicken, onions, peppers and milk in 1-quart microwave-safe bowl. Microwave on High 6 to 7 minutes or until thoroughly heated, stirring every 3 minutes. Cover serving platter with chips; top with chicken mixture and tomatoes.

Nachos de Pollo

■ CRUNCHY ISLAND SPREAD

3 cups

- 1 lb. VELVEETA Pasteurized Process Cheese Spread, cubed
- 1 cup coarsely chopped pecans
- 1 8-oz. can crushed pineapple, drained
- ¼ cup chopped red or green pepper
- 1 tablespoon finely chopped onion

In large bowl of electric mixer, beat process cheese spread at medium speed until smooth. Stir in remaining ingredients. Cover; chill. Serve with crackers.

Preparation time: 10 minutes plus chilling

■ CREAMY HORSERADISH DIPPER

1⅓ cups

- ½ lb. VELVEETA Pasteurized Process Cheese Spread, cubed
- ⅓ cup SAUCEWORKS Horseradish Sauce
- ¼ cup milk

Combine ingredients in saucepan; stir over low heat until process cheese spread is melted. Serve with hot cooked chicken nuggets.

Preparation time: 5 minutes
Cooking time: 10 minutes

Microwave: Microwave ingredients in 1-quart microwave-safe bowl on High 4 to 5 minutes or until process cheese spread is melted, stirring every 2 minutes. Serve with hot cooked chicken nuggets.

"Velveeta" After School Snack

■ "VELVEETA" AFTER SCHOOL SNACK

Approximately 1 dozen

1 cup flour
1 cup graham cracker crumbs
½ cup packed brown sugar
½ teaspoon baking soda
½ cup PARKAY Margarine, melted
2 cups (8 ozs.) VELVEETA Shredded Pasteurized Process Cheese Food
2½ cups peeled apple slices
¼ cup granulated sugar
½ cup coarsely chopped pecans

In medium bowl, combine flour, crumbs, brown sugar and soda. Add margarine; mix well. Reserve ½ cup crumb mixture; press remaining mixture onto bottom of 9-inch square pan. Cover with process cheese food. Combine apples and granulated sugar; mix lightly. Arrange apple mixture on process cheese food. Top with reserved crumb mixture and pecans. Bake at 350°, 35 to 40 minutes or until apples are tender. Cool; cut into bars.

Preparation time: 15 minutes
Baking time: 40 minutes

South-of-the-Border Dip

■ SOUTH-OF-THE-
BORDER DIP

3 cups

½ cup chopped onion
2 tablespoons PARKAY
   Margarine
1 lb. VELVEETA Mexican
   Pasteurized Process Cheese
   Spread with Jalapeño
   Pepper, cubed
1 14½-oz. can tomatoes,
   chopped, drained

In large skillet, saute onions in margarine; reduce heat to low. Add remaining ingredients; stir until process cheese spread is melted. Serve hot with tortilla chips or vegetable dippers.

Preparation time: 10 minutes
Cooking time: 10 minutes

Microwave: Microwave onions and margarine in 1½-quart microwave-safe bowl on High 1½ minutes or until tender. Add remaining ingredients; mix well. Microwave on High 5 minutes or until thoroughly heated, stirring after 3 minutes. Serve hot with tortilla chips or vegetable dippers.

QUICK VEGETABLE DIP

Approximately ¾ cup

    ¼ lb. VELVEETA Pasteurized
        Process Cheese Spread,
        cubed
    ⅓ cup sour cream
    1 tablespoon finely chopped
        green pepper
    1 tablespoon finely chopped
        onion
    1 tablespoon finely chopped
        pimento

In 1-quart saucepan, combine process cheese spread and sour cream; stir over low heat until process cheese spread is melted. Add remaining ingredients; stir. Cover; chill. Serve with assorted vegetable dippers.

Preparation time: 10 minutes
Cooking time: 5 minutes plus
                chilling

Microwave: Microwave process cheese spread and sour cream in 1-quart microwave-safe bowl on High 2 to 3 minutes or until process cheese spread is melted, stirring after every minute. Add remaining ingredients; stir. Cover; chill. Serve with assorted vegetable dippers.

MINI MEXICAN PIZZAS

10 snacks

    1 7½-oz. can PILLSBURY
        Refrigerated Buttermilk
        Biscuits
    ½ cup pizza sauce
    ¼ lb. VELVEETA Mexican
        Pasteurized Process Cheese
        Spread with Jalapeño
        Pepper, cubed
    ½ cup chopped green pepper or
        mushroom slices

Separate dough into ten biscuits. On lightly greased cookie sheet, press each biscuit to form 4-inch circle; pinch edge to form rim. Top each biscuit with 2 teaspoonfuls sauce, spreading to edge. Top with process cheese spread and peppers. Bake at 450°, 6 to 9 minutes or until biscuits are golden brown.

Preparation time: 15 minutes
Baking time: 9 minutes

CLASSIC NACHOS

6 to 8 servings

    1 lb. VELVEETA Pasteurized
        Process Cheese Spread,
        cubed
    ¼ cup picante sauce
        Tortilla chips
    2 cups shredded lettuce
    1 cup chopped tomato
    ¼ cup pitted ripe olive slices

Combine process cheese spread and sauce in saucepan; stir over low heat until process cheese spread is melted. Place chips on serving platter; top with lettuce, process cheese spread mixture, tomatoes and olives.

Preparation time: 10 minutes
Cooking time: 10 minutes

Variation: Substitute VELVEETA Mexican Pasteurized Process Cheese Spread with Jalapeño Pepper for Process Cheese Spread.

Microwave: Combine process cheese spread and sauce in 1-quart microwave-safe bowl. Microwave on High 4 to 5 minutes or until process cheese spread is melted, stirring every 2 minutes. Place chips on serving platter; top with lettuce, process cheese spread mixture, tomatoes and olives.

MAIN DISHES

■ TASTY TACO PIE

4 to 6 servings

> 1 lb. ground beef
> 2 8-oz. cans tomato sauce
> 1 1.25-oz. pkg. taco seasoning mix
> 1 8-oz. can PILLSBURY Refrigerated Quick Crescent Dinner Rolls
> ½ lb. VELVEETA Pasteurized Process Cheese Spread, cubed
> 1 cup shredded lettuce
> ½ cup chopped tomato
> ¼ cup pitted ripe olive slices

Brown meat; drain. Stir in tomato sauce and seasoning mix; simmer 5 minutes. Unroll dough; press onto bottom and sides of ungreased 12-inch pizza pan. Prick bottom and sides with fork. Bake at 375°, 10 to 12 minutes or until golden brown. Cover crust with meat mixture; top with process cheese spread. Continue baking until process cheese spread begins to melt. Top with remaining ingredients. Serve with sour cream, if desired.

Preparation time: 20 minutes
Baking time: 15 minutes

Variation: Substitute VELVEETA Mexican Pasteurized Process Cheese Spread with Jalapeño Pepper for Process Cheese Spread.

Microwave: Crumble meat into 1-quart microwave-safe bowl. Microwave on High 5 to 6 minutes, stirring after 3 minutes; drain. Stir in tomato sauce and seasoning mix. Microwave on High 3 minutes. Continue as directed. Serve with sour cream, if desired.

Tasty Taco Pie

■ TUNA-NOODLE CRISPY

4 to 6 servings

½ lb. VELVEETA Pasteurized
  Process Cheese Spread,
  cubed
1 10¾-oz. can condensed cream
  of mushroom soup
½ cup milk
2 cups (4 ozs.) noodles, cooked,
  drained
1 6½-oz. can tuna, drained,
  flaked
1 2-oz. jar chopped pimento,
  drained
  Dash of pepper
¾ cup coarsely crumbled
  buttery flavored crackers

In 3-quart saucepan, combine process cheese spread, soup and milk;
stir over low heat until smooth. Add
noodles, tuna, pimento and pepper;
mix well. Spoon into 2-quart casserole; top with crackers. Bake at 325°,
20 minutes.

Preparation time: 15 minutes
Baking time: 20 minutes

Microwave: Reduce milk to ¼ cup.
Combine process cheese spread, soup
and milk in 1½-quart microwave-safe
casserole. Microwave on High 4 minutes, stirring after 2 minutes. Stir in
noodles, tuna, pimento and pepper.
Microwave on High 6 to 7 minutes or
until thoroughly heated, stirring every
3 minutes. Top with crackers. Microwave on High 1 minute.

Steak Oriental

■ STEAK ORIENTAL

4 to 6 servings

1 cup diagonally-cut carrot
  slices
1 cup diagonally-cut celery
  slices
1 garlic clove, minced
2 tablespoons oil
1 lb. beef round steak, cut into
  thin strips
1 8-oz. can sliced water
  chestnuts, drained
3 tablespoons soy sauce
½ lb. VELVEETA Pasteurized
  Process Cheese Spread,
  cubed
  Hot cooked rice

In large skillet, stir-fry carrots, celery
and garlic in oil 4 to 5 minutes or
until crisp-tender. Add steak. Cook 3
to 4 minutes, stirring constantly until
steak is tender; drain. Reduce heat to
low. Add water chestnuts, soy sauce
and process cheese spread; stir until
process cheese spread is melted. Serve
over rice.

Preparation time: 20 minutes
Cooking time: 15 minutes

Microwave: Reduce oil to 1 tablespoon. Combine carrots, celery, garlic and oil in 2-quart microwave-safe bowl. Microwave on High 3 to 4 minutes or until crisp-tender. Stir in steak. Microwave on High 5 to 6 minutes, stirring after 3 minutes; drain. Add water chestnuts, soy sauce and process cheese spread. Microwave on High 2 to 2½ minutes or until process cheese spread is melted. Stir. Serve over rice.

■ HAM 'N POTATOES AU GRATIN

4 to 6 servings

¼ cup chopped green pepper
¼ cup chopped onion
1 tablespoon PARKAY Margarine
½ lb. VELVEETA Pasteurized Process Cheese Spread, cubed
¼ cup milk
3 cups cubed cooked potatoes
¾ cup chopped ham

In large skillet, saute peppers and onions in margarine. Reduce heat to low. Add process cheese spread and milk; stir until process cheese spread is melted. Add remaining ingredients; mix well. Heat thoroughly, stirring occasionally.

Preparation time: 30 minutes
Cooking time: 15 minutes

Microwave: Combine peppers, onions and margarine in 1½-quart microwave-safe bowl. Microwave on High 1½ minutes. Add process cheese spread and milk. Microwave on High 2 to 3 minutes or until process cheese spread is melted, stirring after 2 minutes. Stir in remaining ingredients; microwave on High 3 to 4 minutes or until thoroughly heated.

Tostadas Olé

■ TOSTADAS OLÉ

6 servings

6 6-inch flour tortillas
 Oil
½ cup chopped green pepper
2 tablespoons PARKAY
  Margarine
¾ lb. VELVEETA Mexican
  Pasteurized Process Cheese
  Spread with Jalapeño
  Pepper, cubed
¼ cup milk
2 cups cooked chicken strips
 Lettuce
1 8-oz. can kidney beans,
  drained
½ cup chopped tomato

Fry tortillas in ¼-inch hot oil until crisp and golden, turning once; drain. In large skillet, saute peppers in margarine. Reduce heat to low. Add process cheese spread and milk; stir until process cheese spread is melted. Stir in chicken. For each serving, top tortilla with lettuce, chicken mixture, beans and tomatoes.

Preparation time: 15 minutes
Cooking time: 10 minutes

■ CHICKEN ENCHILADA MAGNIFICO

4 servings

- ½ cup chopped onion
- 2 tablespoons PARKAY Margarine
- 2 cups (8 ozs.) VELVEETA Mexican Shredded Pasteurized Process Cheese Food with Jalapeño Pepper
- ½ cup milk
- 2 cups chopped cooked chicken
- ½ cup pitted ripe olive slices
- 8 6-inch flour tortillas Oil
- ½ cup salsa

In large skillet, saute onions in margarine. Add 1½ cups process cheese food and milk. Reduce heat to low. Stir until process cheese food is melted. Add chicken and olives; mix well. Dip tortillas in hot oil to soften; drain. Place ¼ cup chicken mixture in center of each tortilla; roll up. Place, seam side down, in 12×8-inch baking dish; top with salsa. Bake at 350°, 15 minutes or until thoroughly heated. Top with remaining process cheese food and additional pitted ripe olive slices, if desired.

Preparation time: 20 minutes
Baking time: 15 minutes

Microwave: Omit oil. Microwave onions and margarine in 2-quart microwave-safe bowl on High 2 to 4 minutes or until crisp-tender, stirring after 2 minutes. Stir in 1½ cups process cheese food and milk. Microwave on High 5 to 7 minutes or until process cheese food is melted, stirring every 3 minutes. Add chicken and olives; mix well. Wrap tortillas in dampened paper towels. Microwave on High 1 to 2 minutes or until softened. Assemble recipe as directed. Cover with plastic wrap; vent. Microwave on High 3 minutes or until thoroughly heated, turning dish after 1½ minutes. Top with remaining process cheese food and additional pitted ripe olive slices, if desired.

■ QUICHE FLORENTINE

6 to 8 servings

- 1 15-oz. pkg. PILLSBURY All Ready Pie Crust
- 2 cups (8 ozs.) VELVEETA Shredded Pasteurized Process Cheese Food
- ⅓ cup (1½ ozs.) KRAFT 100% Grated Parmesan Cheese
- 1 10-oz. pkg. frozen chopped spinach, thawed, well-drained
- 4 crisply cooked bacon slices, crumbled
- ¾ cup milk
- 3 eggs, beaten
- ¼ teaspoon pepper

Prepare pie crust according to package directions for filled one-crust pie using 9-inch pie plate. (Refrigerate remaining crust for later use.) In large bowl, combine remaining ingredients; mix well. Pour into unbaked pie crust. Bake at 350°, 35 to 40 minutes or until knife inserted in center comes out clean. Let stand 10 minutes before serving.

Preparation time: 15 minutes
Baking time: 40 minutes plus
standing

■ SAVORY SALMON STEAKS

4 servings

4 ½-inch-thick salmon steaks
½ cup dry white wine
2 tablespoons green onion
  slices

* * *

½ lb. VELVEETA Pasteurized
  Process Cheese Spread,
  cubed
3 tablespoons dry white wine
¼ teaspoon dried tarragon
  leaves, crushed
¼ teaspoon dill weed

Place fish in 9-inch square baking dish; top with wine and onions. Cover; bake at 350°, 30 to 35 minutes or until fish flakes easily with fork.

Combine remaining ingredients in saucepan; stir over low heat until process cheese spread is melted. Serve with fish.

Preparation time: 10 minutes
Baking time: 35 minutes

Variation: Substitute apple juice for wine.

Microwave: Decrease wine to ⅓ cup for fish and 2 tablespoons for sauce. Place fish in 9-inch square microwave-safe dish; top with wine and onions. Cover with plastic wrap; vent. Microwave on High 6 to 8 minutes or until fish flakes easily with fork, turning dish every 2 minutes.

Combine remaining ingredients in 1-quart microwave-safe bowl. Microwave on High 3 to 4 minutes or until process cheese spread is melted, stirring after 2 minutes. Serve with fish.

■ FIESTA CHICKEN

4 servings

1 cup fresh bread crumbs
¼ cup (1 oz.) KRAFT 100% Grated
  Parmesan Cheese
1 teaspoon chili powder
¼ teaspoon ground cumin
¼ teaspoon garlic powder
¼ teaspoon ground oregano
2 whole chicken breasts, split,
  boned, skinned
¼ lb. VELVEETA Mexican
  Pasteurized Process Cheese
  Spread with Jalapeño
  Pepper, cubed
½ cup PARKAY Margarine,
  melted

Combine crumbs, parmesan cheese and seasonings. Cut slit along side of each chicken breast to form pocket. Fill each pocket with process cheese spread. Close opening with wooden picks. Dip in margarine; coat with crumb mixture. Place in shallow baking dish. Sprinkle any remaining crumb mixture over chicken; drizzle any remaining margarine on top. Bake at 400°, 25 minutes or until chicken is tender.

Preparation time: 20 minutes
Baking time: 25 minutes

Savory Salmon Steaks

Omelet Olé

◼ OMELET OLÉ

2 servings

¼ cup chopped red pepper
2 tablespoons green onion
    slices
2 tablespoons PARKAY
    Margarine
3 eggs, beaten
2 tablespoons milk
¼ lb. VELVEETA Mexican
    Pasteurized Process Cheese
    Spread with Jalapeño
    Pepper, cubed

Saute peppers and onions in 1 table-spoon margarine in 7-inch skillet. Remove vegetables from skillet. Melt remaining margarine in skillet over low heat. Add combined eggs and milk. As eggs set, lift edges slightly with spatula to allow uncooked portion to flow underneath. When eggs are set but top is still moist, place ½ cup process cheese spread and ¼ cup vegetables on half of omelet. Slip spatula underneath, tip skillet to loosen and gently fold in half. Top with remaining process cheese spread and vegetables. Cover 2 to 3 minutes or until process cheese spread begins to melt.

Preparation time: 10 minutes
Cooking time: 10 minutes

Microwave: Microwave peppers, onions and 1 tablespoon margarine in 9-inch microwave-safe pie plate on High 1 minute. Remove vegetables from pie plate. Microwave remaining margarine in pie plate on High 30 seconds or until melted. Add combined eggs and milk. Microwave on

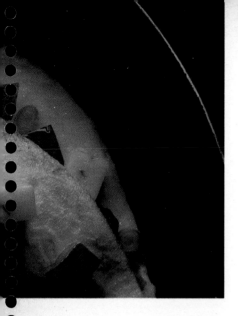

■ ITALIAN ZUCCHINI BAKE

6 servings

1 lb. bulk pork sausage
½ cup sour cream
½ lb. VELVEETA Pasteurized Process Cheese Spread, cubed
¼ cup dry bread crumbs
1 teaspoon dried oregano leaves
3 cups thin zucchini slices

In large skillet, brown sausage; drain. Stir in sour cream, ¼ lb. process cheese spread, crumbs and oregano. Cover bottom of 10×6-inch baking dish with zucchini; top with sausage mixture and remaining process cheese spread. Bake at 350°, 25 minutes. Serve over hot cooked pasta, if desired.

Preparation time: 15 minutes
Baking time: 25 minutes

Microwave: Crumble sausage into 1½-quart microwave-safe bowl. Microwave on High 6 to 7 minutes, stirring after 3 minutes; drain. Combine with sour cream, ¼ lb. process cheese spread, crumbs and oregano. Cover bottom of 10×6-inch microwave-safe dish with zucchini. Cover with plastic wrap; vent. Microwave on High 2 minutes. Top with sausage mixture. Microwave on High, uncovered, 5 minutes. Top with remaining process cheese spread. Microwave on High 1 to 2 minutes or until process cheese spread begins to melt. Serve over hot cooked pasta, if desired.

High 3 to 4 minutes or until eggs are set but top is still moist, lifting edges slightly with spatula to allow uncooked portion to flow underneath after each minute. Place ½ cup process cheese spread and ¼ cup vegetables on half of omelet. Slip spatula underneath, tip pie plate to loosen and gently fold in half. Top with remaining process cheese spread and vegetables. Microwave on High 1 to 1½ minutes or until process cheese spread begins to melt.

■ TURKEY SAUTÉ

4 servings

1 lb. turkey tenderloin, cut into
   1-inch cubes
1 garlic clove, minced
2 tablespoons PARKAY
   Margarine
3 cups frozen mixed vegetables
¾ lb. VELVEETA Pasteurized
   Process Cheese Spread,
   cubed
4 cups hot cooked rice
⅓ cup coarsely chopped pecans

In large skillet, cook turkey and garlic in margarine over low heat 5 minutes, stirring occasionally. Stir in vegetables; continue cooking 10 to 15
minutes or until vegetables are tender, stirring occasionally. Add process cheese spread; stir until melted.
Serve over rice. Top with pecans.

Preparation time: 10 minutes
Cooking time: 25 minutes

Microwave: Combine turkey, garlic
and margarine in 2-quart microwave-
safe bowl; microwave on High 5 minutes, stirring every 2 minutes. Add
vegetables; mix lightly. Microwave on
High 8 to 9 minutes or until thoroughly heated, stirring after 5 minutes; drain. Add process cheese
spread. Microwave on High 2 to 3
minutes or until process cheese
spread is melted, stirring after 2
minutes. Serve over rice. Top with
pecans.

■ DILLED SALMON LOAF

6 servings

¼ lb. VELVEETA Pasteurized
   Process Cheese Spread,
   cubed
¼ cup milk
1 15½-oz. can salmon, drained,
   skinned, boned, flaked
2 eggs, beaten
⅔ cup dry bread crumbs
½ cup finely chopped celery
½ cup finely chopped onion
1 tablespoon lemon juice
½ teaspoon dill weed
        *   *   *
½ lb. VELVEETA Pasteurized
   Process Cheese Spread,
   cubed
¼ cup milk
1 2¼-oz. can sliced ripe olives,
   drained

In large saucepan, combine process
cheese spread and milk; stir over low
heat until process cheese spread is
melted. Add salmon, eggs, crumbs,
celery, onions, juice and dill; mix
well. Place in greased 8×4-inch loaf
pan. Bake at 350°, 40 to 45 minutes
or until golden brown.

Combine process cheese spread and
milk in saucepan, stirring over low
heat until process cheese spread is
melted. Stir in olives. Serve over
salmon.

Preparation time: 20 minutes
Baking time: 45 minutes

Microwave: Prepare and bake salmon loaf as directed. Microwave process cheese spread and milk in 2-cup
microwave-safe measure on High 3 to
4 minutes or until process cheese
spread is melted, stirring after 2 minutes. Stir in olives. Microwave on High
30 seconds to 1 minute or until thoroughly heated. Serve over salmon.

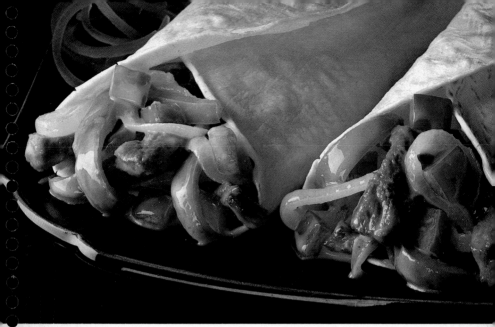

Festive Fajitas

■ FESTIVE FAJITAS

4 servings

1 lb. beef round steak, cut into
  thin strips
2 tablespoons oil
1 medium green pepper, cut
  into strips
1 medium onion, sliced
¼ lb. VELVEETA Mexican
  Pasteurized Process Cheese
  Spread with Jalapeño
  Pepper, cubed
4 8-inch flour tortillas
1 cup chopped tomato

In large skillet, saute steak in oil 4
minutes. Add peppers and onions; mix
lightly. Reduce heat to medium. Cook
5 minutes or until steak is tender;
drain. Add process cheese spread; stir
until melted. Fill tortillas with steak
mixture and tomatoes.

Preparation time: 20 minutes
Cooking time: 20 minutes

Variation: Substitute 2 whole chick-
en breasts, split, boned, skinned, cut
into strips, for 1 lb. beef round steak.

Microwave: Reduce oil to 1 tablespoon. Microwave steak and oil in 1½-
quart microwave-safe bowl on High
4 to 6 minutes, stirring after 3 minutes. Stir in peppers and onions. Microwave on High 4 to 6 minutes or
until vegetables are crisp-tender, stirring every 2 minutes. Add process
cheese spread. Microwave on High 2
to 2½ minutes or until process cheese
spread is melted. Stir. Fill tortillas
with steak mixture and tomatoes.

Regal Shrimp on Rice

■ REGAL SHRIMP ON RICE

6 servings

3 cups cooked rice
1 cup milk
2 eggs, beaten
¼ cup (1 oz.) KRAFT 100% Grated
   Parmesan Cheese
2 tablespoons green onion
   slices

      *   *   *

2 cups mushroom slices
½ cup green pepper strips
2 tablespoons PARKAY
   Margarine
1 lb. frozen cleaned shrimp,
   cooked, drained
¾ lb. VELVEETA Pasteurized
   Process Cheese Spread,
   cubed
¼ cup dry white wine
½ teaspoon dried tarragon
   leaves, crushed

In large bowl, combine rice, milk, eggs, parmesan cheese and onions; mix well. Spoon into greased 9-inch pie plate. Bake at 350°, 35 to 40 minutes or until knife inserted near center comes out clean. Cut into wedges.

Saute mushrooms and peppers in margarine. Reduce heat to medium. Add remaining ingredients; stir until process cheese spread is melted. Serve over rice wedges.

Preparation time: 20 minutes
Baking time: 40 minutes

Variation: Substitute milk for wine.

Microwave: Combine rice, milk, eggs, parmesan cheese and onions; mix well. Spoon into greased 9-inch microwave-safe pie plate. Microwave on High 10 to 12 minutes or until rice mixture is just set, turning dish after 6 minutes. Cut into wedges.

Reduce margarine to 1 tablespoon and wine to 2 tablespoons. Combine mushrooms, peppers and margarine in 2-quart microwave-safe bowl. Cover with plastic wrap; vent. Microwave on High 3 to 3½ minutes or until mushrooms are tender. Add remaining ingredients. Cover with plastic wrap; vent. Microwave on High 2 to 3 minutes or until process cheese spread is melted. Serve over rice wedges.

■ BEEF NOODLE BAKE

4 to 6 servings

1 lb. ground beef
1 8-oz. can tomato sauce
⅓ cup chopped onion
2 tablespoons chopped green pepper
4 cups (8 ozs.) noodles, cooked, drained
½ lb. VELVEETA Pasteurized Process Cheese Spread, cubed

In large skillet, brown meat; drain. Add sauce, onions and peppers; mix well. Cover; simmer 5 minutes. Layer noodles, process cheese spread and meat mixture in 1½-quart casserole; cover. Bake at 350°, 40 minutes. Top with additional process cheese spread, sliced, if desired.

Preparation time: 15 minutes
Baking time: 40 minutes

Variation: Substitute 2 cups (7 ozs.) elbow macaroni, cooked, drained, for 4 cups noodles.

Microwave: Crumble meat into 1-quart microwave-safe bowl; stir in onions and peppers. Microwave on High 5 to 6 minutes, stirring after 3 minutes; drain. Stir in sauce; microwave on High 2 minutes. Layer noodles, process cheese spread and meat mixture in 1½-quart microwave-safe casserole. Cover with plastic wrap; vent. Microwave on High 2 to 3 minutes or until thoroughly heated. Top with additional process cheese spread, sliced, if desired.

TEX-MEX MEAT SQUARES

6 servings

1 lb. ground beef
1 cup salsa
¼ cup chopped onion
½ teaspoon ground cumin
2 tablespoons cornmeal
1 10-oz. can PILLSBURY Pipin' Hot® Refrigerated White Loaf
1 cup (4 ozs.) VELVEETA Mexican Shredded Pasteurized Process Cheese Food with Jalapeño Pepper

Brown meat; drain. Stir in salsa, onions and cumin. Sprinkle 13×9-inch pan with cornmeal. Unroll dough; press evenly into pan, sealing perforations. Spread meat mixture over dough. Bake at 375°, 25 minutes. Top with process cheese food; continue baking until process cheese food begins to melt.

Preparation time: 15 minutes
Baking time: 30 minutes

CHEESY CHILI TATERS

6 servings

1 lb. ground beef
⅓ cup chopped onion
1 8-oz. can kidney beans, drained
1 cup cold water
½ cup KRAFT Barbecue Sauce
1 tablespoon chili powder
6 hot baked potatoes, partially split
1 cup (4 ozs.) VELVEETA Shredded Pasteurized Process Cheese Food

Brown meat; drain. Add onions; cook until tender. Stir in beans, water, barbecue sauce and chili powder; simmer 15 minutes, stirring occasionally. Top potatoes with chili mixture and process cheese food.

Preparation time: 60 minutes
Cooking time: 15 minutes

Microwave: Omit water. Crumble meat into 1½-quart microwave-safe bowl. Microwave on High 5 to 6 minutes, stirring after 3 minutes; drain. Stir in onions, beans, barbecue sauce and chili powder. Microwave on High 6 to 8 minutes or until thoroughly heated, stirring every 3 minutes. Top potatoes with chili mixture and process cheese food.

MEAT LOAF ITALIANO

6 servings

1 egg, beaten
1½ lbs. ground beef
1 8-oz. can pizza sauce
¾ cup (3 ozs.) VELVEETA Shredded Pasteurized Process Cheese Food
¾ cup old fashioned or quick oats, uncooked
¼ cup cold water
½ teaspoon dried oregano leaves, crushed

In large bowl, combine all ingredients except ¼ cup sauce; mix lightly. Shape into loaf in 10×6-inch baking dish. Bake at 350°, 1 hour. Top with remaining sauce. Let stand 10 minutes before serving.

Preparation time: 10 minutes
Baking time: 60 minutes plus standing

Chicken Puff Bravo

■ CHICKEN PUFF BRAVO

8 servings

    ¾ lb. VELVEETA Mexican
        Pasteurized Process Cheese
        Spread with Jalapeño
        Pepper, cubed
    ½ cup sour cream
    ¼ teaspoon garlic salt
     2 eggs, separated
     2 10-oz. pkgs. frozen chopped
        spinach, thawed, well-
        drained
     3 cups chopped cooked chicken
    ¼ cup chopped red or green
        pepper
     1 4-oz. can sliced mushrooms,
        drained
     2 8-oz. cans PILLSBURY
        Refrigerated Quick Crescent
        Dinner Rolls

In 3-quart saucepan, combine process cheese spread, sour cream and
garlic salt; stir over low heat until
process cheese spread is melted. Remove from heat. Beat egg yolks thoroughly; reserve 1 tablespoon for
glaze. Gradually stir remaining egg
yolks into cheese mixture. Cool. Beat
egg whites until stiff peaks form; fold
into cheese mixture. Add remaining
ingredients except dough; mix lightly. Unroll one can dough; press onto
bottom and sides of greased 12-inch
ovenproof skillet, pressing perforations together to seal. Spread spinach
mixture over dough. Unroll second
can dough; separate into eight triangles. Loosely twist each triangle at
pointed end. Arrange dough triangles
on spinach mixture, pointed ends to-
wards center. Seal outer edges to
crust. Brush dough with reserved egg
yolk. Bake at 375°, 35 to 40 minutes
or until egg mixture is set.

Preparation time: 20 minutes
Baking time: 40 minutes

Variation: Substitute 2-oz. jar sliced
pimento, drained, for red or green
pepper.

Recipe Tip: Substitute 12-inch deep-
dish pizza pan for skillet.

Saucy Stuffed Chicken Breast

■ SAUCY STUFFED CHICKEN BREAST

4 servings

1 8¾-oz. can whole kernel corn,
   drained
¼ cup shredded zucchini
½ cup MIRACLE WHIP Salad
   Dressing
2 whole chicken breasts, split
1 cup buttery cracker crumbs
         *   *   *
½ lb. VELVEETA Pasteurized
   Process Cheese Spread,
   cubed
⅓ cup MIRACLE WHIP Salad
   Dressing
3 tablespoons milk
¼ cup shredded zucchini

Combine vegetables and ¼ cup salad dressing; mix lightly. Loosen skin of each chicken breast to form pocket; fill with vegetable mixture. Close opening with wooden picks. Brush chicken with ¼ cup salad dressing; coat with crumbs. Place in 12×8-inch baking dish. Bake at 350°, 55 minutes or until tender.

Combine process cheese spread, salad dressing and milk in saucepan; stir over low heat until process cheese spread is melted. Stir in zucchini; serve over chicken.

Preparation time: 30 minutes
Baking time: 55 minutes

SOUTHWESTERN EGG PUFF

4 to 6 servings

1 lb. VELVEETA Mexican Pasteurized Process Cheese Spread with Jalapeño Pepper, cubed
2 cups cottage cheese
6 eggs, beaten
½ cup picante sauce
¼ cup PARKAY Margarine, melted
¼ cup flour
½ teaspoon baking powder
½ teaspoon seasoned salt
1 12-oz. can whole kernel corn with sweet peppers, drained

In large bowl, combine ingredients; mix well. Pour into greased 12×8-inch baking dish. Bake at 350°, 35 to 40 minutes or until golden brown. Top with additional picante sauce, sour cream and avocado slices, if desired.

Preparation time: 10 minutes
Baking time: 40 minutes

Variation: Substitute VELVEETA Pasteurized Process Cheese Spread for Process Cheese Spread with Jalapeño Pepper.

SPANISH CHOPS

4 servings

4 pork chops
1 tablespoon oil
1 14½-oz. can tomatoes, cut up, undrained
1 garlic clove, minced
1 teaspoon ground cumin
½ lb. VELVEETA Mexican Pasteurized Process Cheese Spread with Jalapeño Pepper, sliced

Brown chops in oil; drain. Combine tomatoes, garlic and cumin; pour over chops. Cover; simmer 35 to 40 minutes or until chops are done. Top with process cheese spread; continue cooking until process cheese spread is melted. Top with peeled avocado slices, if desired.

Preparation time: 10 minutes
Cooking time: 50 minutes

CHILI CORN CHIP BAKE

4 to 6 servings

4 cups corn chips
2 15-oz. cans chili without beans, heated
½ lb. VELVEETA Pasteurized Process Cheese Spread, sliced

Layer half of chips, chili and process cheese spread in 10×6-inch baking dish; repeat layers of chips and chili. Bake at 350°, 30 minutes. Top with remaining process cheese spread; continue baking until process cheese spread begins to melt.

Preparation time: 10 minutes
Baking time: 35 minutes

Variation: Substitute VELVEETA Mexican Pasteurized Process Cheese Spread with Jalapeño Pepper for Process Cheese Spread.

Microwave: Prepare recipe as directed in 10×6-inch microwave-safe dish. Microwave on High 5 to 6 minutes or until thoroughly heated, turning dish after 3 minutes. Top with remaining process cheese spread. Microwave on High 1½ to 2 minutes or until process cheese spread begins to melt.

GOLDEN CHICKEN AND RICE

4 to 6 servings

1 2½- to 3-lb. broiler-fryer,
    cut up
1 10¾-oz. can condensed cream
    of mushroom soup
¾ lb. VELVEETA Pasteurized
    Process Cheese Spread,
    cubed
2¼ cups uncooked instant rice
½ cup cold water
⅓ cup chopped onion
1 2-oz. jar chopped pimento,
    drained
    Paprika

Remove skin and excess fat from chicken. In 2-quart saucepan, combine soup and process cheese spread; stir over low heat until process cheese spread is melted. Add rice, water, onions and pimento; mix well. Spoon into 13×9-inch baking dish. Place chicken on top of rice mixture; cover. Bake at 350°, 45 minutes. Uncover; sprinkle with paprika. Continue baking 15 minutes or until chicken is tender.

Preparation time: 20 minutes
Baking time: 60 minutes

Microwave: Reduce water to ¼ cup. Remove skin and excess fat from chicken. In 12×8-inch microwave-safe dish, combine soup, process cheese spread, rice, water, onions and pimento; mix well. Place chicken on top of rice mixture. Cover with plastic wrap; vent. Microwave on High 20 to 22 minutes or until chicken is tender, turning dish after 10 minutes. Uncover; sprinkle with paprika. Microwave on High 1½ to 2½ minutes. Let stand 5 minutes.

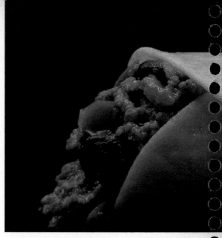

Enchiladas Acapulco

ENCHILADAS ACAPULCO

4 servings

1 lb. ground beef
1 8-oz. can tomato sauce
¾ cup chopped green pepper
1 8¾-oz. can kidney beans,
    drained
½ lb. VELVEETA Mexican
    Pasteurized Process Cheese
    Spread with Jalapeño
    Pepper, cubed
8 6-inch tortillas
    Oil
½ cup chopped tomato

In large skillet, brown meat; drain. Add sauce and ½ cup peppers; cook over medium heat 5 minutes, stirring occasionally. Add beans and ¼ lb. process cheese spread; continue cooking until process cheese spread is melted. Dip tortillas in hot oil to soften; drain. Fill each tortilla with ¼ cup meat mixture; roll up. Place, seam side down, in 12×8-inch baking dish. Top with remaining meat mixture; cover. Bake at 350°, 20 minutes. Top with remaining process cheese spread; continue baking un-

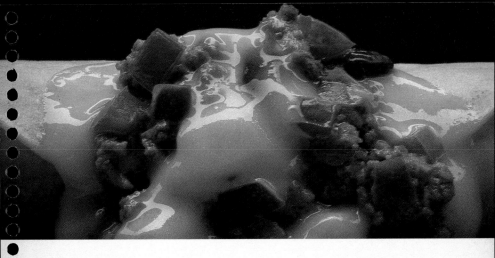

covered 5 to 8 minutes or until process cheese spread is melted. Top with tomatoes and remaining peppers.

Preparation time: 25 minutes
Baking time: 28 minutes

Variation: Substitute VELVEETA Pasteurized Process Cheese Spread for Process Cheese Spread with Jalapeño Pepper.

Microwave: Omit oil. Crumble meat into 1½-quart microwave-safe bowl. Microwave on High 5 to 6 minutes, stirring after 3 minutes; drain. Stir in sauce and ½ cup peppers. Microwave on High 2 minutes. Stir in beans and ¼ lb. process cheese spread. Microwave on High 1 minute; stir until process cheese spread is melted. Wrap tortillas in dampened paper towels. Microwave on High 1 to 2 minutes or until softened. Assemble recipe as directed. Cover with plastic wrap; vent. Microwave on High 3 minutes or until thoroughly heated, turning dish after 1½ minutes. Top with remaining process cheese spread. Cover with plastic wrap; vent. Microwave on High 1 minute or until process cheese spread begins to melt. Top with tomatoes and remaining peppers.

■ SENSATIONAL SCRAMBLED EGGS

4 servings

> 1 tablespoon PARKAY Margarine
> 6 eggs, beaten
> ¼ lb. VELVEETA Pasteurized Process Cheese Spread, cubed

Melt margarine in skillet over low heat. Add eggs and process cheese spread. Cook slowly, stirring occasionally, until eggs are set and process cheese spread is melted.

Preparation time: 5 minutes
Cooking time: 10 minutes

Microwave: Microwave margarine in 1½-quart microwave-safe bowl on High 30 seconds or until melted. Add eggs. Microwave on High 2 to 4 minutes or until eggs begin to set, stirring every 1½ minutes. Stir in process cheese spread. Microwave on High 2 to 4 minutes or until eggs are almost set, stirring every 1½ minutes. Let stand 2 minutes; stir.

PASTA

■ SHRIMP MILANO

4 to 6 servings

> 1 lb. frozen cleaned shrimp,
>   cooked, drained
> 2 cups mushroom slices
> 1 cup green or red pepper strips
> 1 garlic clove, minced
> ¼ cup PARKAY Margarine
> ¾ lb. VELVEETA Pasteurized
>   Process Cheese Spread,
>   cubed
> ¾ cup whipping cream
> ½ teaspoon dill weed
> ⅓ cup (1½ ozs.) KRAFT 100%
>   Grated Parmesan Cheese
> 8 ozs. fettucini, cooked, drained

In large skillet, saute shrimp, vegetables and garlic in margarine. Reduce heat to low. Add process cheese spread, cream and dill. Stir until process cheese spread is melted. Stir in parmesan cheese. Add fettucini; toss lightly.

Preparation time: 20 minutes
Cooking time: 15 minutes

Shrimp Milano

■ PASTA VEGETABLE MEDLEY

4 to 6 servings

2 cups broccoli flowerets
2 cups mushroom slices
1 medium red or green pepper,
   cut into strips
2 tablespoons PARKAY
   Margarine
½ lb. VELVEETA Mexican
   Pasteurized Process Cheese
   Spread with Jalapeño
   Pepper, cubed
1 tablespoon milk
1½ cups (6 ozs.) tri-color
   corkscrew noodles, cooked,
   drained

In large skillet, stir-fry vegetables in margarine until crisp-tender. Reduce heat to low. Add process cheese spread and milk; stir until process cheese spread is melted. Add noodles; toss lightly.

Preparation time: 15 minutes
Cooking time: 15 minutes

Microwave: Microwave broccoli, peppers and margarine in 1½-quart microwave-safe casserole on High 2 to 3 minutes or until vegetables are crisp-tender. Add mushrooms. Microwave 2 minutes; drain. Add process cheese spread and milk. Microwave on High 2 to 3 minutes or until process cheese spread is melted, stirring after 2 minutes. Add noodles; toss lightly.

■ SAN FRANCISCO STIR-FRY

4 to 6 servings

1 cup carrot slices
¼ lb. pea pods
½ teaspoon dried tarragon
   leaves, crushed
2 tablespoons PARKAY
   Margarine
¾ lb. VELVEETA Pasteurized
   Process Cheese Spread,
   cubed
¼ cup milk
6 ozs. linguine, cooked, drained

In large skillet, stir-fry vegetables and tarragon in margarine until crisp-tender. Reduce heat to low. Add process cheese spread and milk; stir until process cheese spread is melted. Add linguine; toss lightly.

Preparation time: 10 minutes
Cooking time: 15 minutes

Microwave: In 1½-quart microwave-safe bowl, microwave vegetables, tarragon and margarine on High 3 to 5 minutes or until crisp-tender, stirring every 2 minutes. Stir in process cheese spread and milk; microwave on High 2 to 4 minutes or until process cheese spread is melted, stirring after 2 minutes. Add linguine; toss lightly.

■ LASAGNA ITALIANO

6 to 8 servings

1½ lbs. ground beef
½ cup chopped onion
 1 14½-oz. can tomatoes, cut up
 1 6-oz. can tomato paste
⅓ cup cold water
 1 garlic clove, minced
 1 teaspoon dried oregano
   leaves, crushed
¼ teaspoon pepper
 6 ozs. lasagna noodles, cooked,
   drained
 2 6-oz. pkgs. 100% Natural
   KRAFT Low Moisture Part-
   Skim Mozzarella Cheese
   Slices
½ lb. VELVEETA Pasteurized
   Process Cheese Spread,
   thinly sliced
½ cup (2 ozs.) KRAFT 100%
   Grated Parmesan Cheese

In large skillet, brown meat; drain. Add onions; cook until tender. Stir in tomatoes, tomato paste, water, garlic and seasonings. Cover; simmer 30 minutes. In 12×8-inch baking dish, layer half of noodles, meat sauce, mozzarella cheese, process cheese spread and parmesan cheese; repeat layers. Bake at 350°, 30 minutes. Let stand 10 minutes before serving.

Preparation time: 40 minutes
Baking time: 30 minutes plus
standing

Vegetables Fromage

■ VEGETABLES FROMAGE

4 to 6 servings

  2 **cups julienne-cut carrots**
  2 **cups julienne-cut zucchini**
  1 **medium green pepper, cut
     into strips**
  1 **garlic clove, minced**
  3 **tablespoons PARKAY
     Margarine**
 ½ **lb. VELVEETA Pasteurized
     Process Cheese Spread,
     cubed**
 ¼ **cup half and half**
  1 **teaspoon dried basil leaves,
     crushed**
1½ **cups (6 ozs.) bow noodles,
     cooked, drained**

In large skillet, stir-fry carrots, zucchini, peppers and garlic in margarine until crisp-tender. Reduce heat to low. Add process cheese spread, half and half and basil; stir until process cheese spread is melted. Add noodles; mix lightly. Heat thoroughly, stirring occasionally.

*Preparation time: 20 minutes
Cooking time: 10 minutes*

Variations: Substitute milk for half and half.

Substitute corkscrew noodles for bow noodles.

Substitute 2 tablespoons chopped fresh basil leaves for dried basil.

■ SANTA FE PASTA

6 servings

- ¾ lb. VELVEETA Pasteurized Process Cheese Spread
- 2 tablespoons milk
- 1 8¾-oz. can whole kernel corn, drained
- 1 8-oz. can kidney beans, drained
- 2 cups (8 ozs.) mostaccioli noodles, cooked, drained
- 1 4-oz. can chopped green chilies, drained
- ½ teaspoon chili powder
- 1 cup corn chips

Cube ½ lb. process cheese spread. In large saucepan, combine with milk; stir over low heat until process cheese spread is melted. Add corn, beans, noodles, chilies and chili powder; mix lightly. Spoon mixture into 1½-quart casserole. Bake at 350°, 20 minutes. Top with chips and remaining process cheese spread, sliced. Continue baking until process cheese spread begins to melt.

Preparation time: 15 minutes
Baking time: 25 minutes

Microwave: Cube ½ lb. process cheese spread. Combine with milk in 2-quart microwave-safe bowl. Microwave on High 2 to 3 minutes or until process cheese spread is melted, stirring after 2 minutes. Stir in corn, beans, noodles, chilies and chili powder; microwave on High 5 minutes, stirring every 2 minutes. Top with chips and remaining process cheese spread, sliced. Microwave on High 2 minutes or until process cheese spread begins to melt.

Microwave: In 2-quart microwave-safe bowl, microwave carrots, zucchini, peppers, garlic and margarine on High 3 to 4 minutes or until vegetables are crisp-tender. Add process cheese spread, half and half and basil. Microwave on High 2 minutes or until process cheese spread is melted. Add noodles; mix lightly.

Confetti Mac 'n Cheese

■ CONFETTI MAC 'N CHEESE

6 servings

   ¼ **cup chopped onion**
   ½ **cup chopped green pepper**
   2 **tablespoons PARKAY Margarine**
   1 **lb. VELVEETA Pasteurized Process Cheese Spread, cubed**
   ½ **cup milk**
   2 **cups (7 ozs.) elbow macaroni, cooked, drained**

Saute vegetables in margarine until tender. Reduce heat to low. Add process cheese spread and milk; stir until process cheese spread is melted. Stir in macaroni. Spoon into 2-quart casserole. Bake at 350°, 15 minutes. Sprinkle with parmesan cheese, if desired.

Preparation time: 15 minutes
Baking time: 15 minutes

Microwave: Microwave vegetables and margarine in 2½-quart microwave-safe bowl on High 2 to 2½ minutes or until tender. Stir in process cheese spread and milk; microwave on High 3 to 4 minutes or until process cheese spread is melted, stirring after 2 minutes. Add macaroni; toss lightly. Sprinkle with parmesan cheese, if desired.

■ NOUVELLE FETTUCINI

6 servings

- 2 cups broccoli flowerets
- 1 cup carrot slices
- ¼ cup PARKAY Margarine
- 2 cups summer squash slices
- ½ lb. asparagus spears, cut into 1-inch pieces
- 1 teaspoon dried oregano leaves, crushed
- ¾ lb. VELVEETA Pasteurized Process Cheese Spread, cubed
- ¾ cup half and half
- ¼ lb. pepperoni, chopped
- ⅓ cup (1½ ozs.) KRAFT 100% Grated Parmesan Cheese
- 8 ozs. fettucini, cooked, drained

In large skillet, stir-fry broccoli and carrots in margarine 3 minutes. Add squash, asparagus and oregano; stir-fry until crisp-tender. Reduce heat to low. Add process cheese spread, half and half, pepperoni and parmesan cheese; stir until process cheese spread is melted. Add fettucini; toss lightly.

Preparation time: 25 minutes
Cooking time: 15 minutes

Microwave: Reduce half and half to ½ cup. Microwave broccoli, carrots and margarine in 2½-quart microwave-safe bowl on High 2 minutes, stirring after 1 minute. Stir in squash, asparagus and oregano; microwave on High 2 to 3 minutes or until crisp-tender, stirring after 2 minutes. Add process cheese spread and half and half; mix lightly. Microwave on High 4 to 6 minutes or until process cheese spread is melted, stirring every 2 minutes. Stir in pepperoni and parmesan cheese; microwave on High 2 to 4 minutes or until thoroughly heated, stirring after 2 minutes. Add fettucini; toss lightly.

Nouvelle Fettucini

TUNA LASAGNA

6 to 8 servings

½ cup chopped onion
1 garlic clove, minced
1 tablespoon oil
2 6½-oz. cans tuna, drained,
  flaked
1 10¾-oz. can condensed cream
  of celery soup
½ cup milk
½ teaspoon dried oregano
  leaves, crushed
¼ teaspoon pepper
8 ozs. lasagna noodles, cooked,
  drained
1 6-oz. pkg. 100% Natural KRAFT
  Low Moisture Part-Skim
  Mozzarella Cheese Slices
½ lb. VELVEETA Pasteurized
  Process Cheese Spread,
  sliced
¼ cup (1 oz.) KRAFT 100% Grated
  Parmesan Cheese

In large skillet, saute onions and garlic in oil. Stir in tuna, soup, milk and
seasonings. In 12×8-inch baking dish,
layer half of noodles, mozzarella
cheese, tuna mixture, process cheese
spread and parmesan cheese; repeat
layers. Bake at 350°, 30 minutes. Let
stand 10 minutes before serving.

Preparation time: 20 minutes
Baking time: 30 minutes plus
standing

Savory Cheese Tortellini

SAVORY CHEESE TORTELLINI

4 servings

½ lb. VELVEETA Pasteurized
  Process Cheese Spread,
  cubed
¼ cup milk
¼ teaspoon ground nutmeg
1 7-oz. pkg. cheese-filled
  tortellini, cooked, drained

Combine process cheese spread, milk
and nutmeg in saucepan. Stir over low
heat until process cheese spread is
melted. Add tortellini; mix lightly.
Garnish with tomato rose and fresh
basil, if desired.

Preparation time: 10 minutes
Cooking time: 10 minutes

Microwave: Combine process cheese
spread, milk and nutmeg in 1-quart
microwave-safe bowl. Microwave on
High 2½ to 4½ minutes or until process cheese spread is melted, stirring
after 2 minutes. Add tortellini; mix
lightly. Garnish with tomato rose and
fresh basil, if desired.

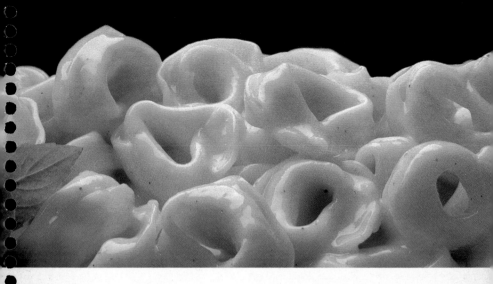

■ SPAGHETTI WITH CREAM SAUCE

6 servings

2 cups mushroom slices
1 cup halved zucchini slices
1 garlic clove, minced
2 tablespoons PARKAY
    Margarine
⅓ cup half and half
½ lb. VELVEETA Pasteurized
    Process Cheese Spread,
    cubed
8 ozs. spaghetti, cooked,
    drained

In large skillet, saute vegetables and garlic in margarine until zucchini is crisp-tender. Reduce heat to low. Add half and half and process cheese spread; stir until process cheese spread is melted. Toss with hot spaghetti.

Preparation time: 15 minutes
Cooking time: 10 minutes

■ SAVORY NOODLES

4 to 6 servings

4 cups (8 ozs.) noodles, cooked,
    drained
½ lb. VELVEETA Pasteurized
    Process Cheese Spread,
    cubed
1 3-oz. pkg. PHILADELPHIA
    BRAND Cream Cheese,
    cubed
½ cup milk
¼ cup chopped onion
    Dash of pepper

In large saucepan, combine ingredients; stir over low heat until process cheese spread is melted.

Preparation time: 15 minutes
Cooking time: 10 minutes

Microwave: Combine all ingredients except noodles in 2-quart microwave-safe bowl. Microwave on High 6 to 7 minutes or until process cheese spread is melted, stirring every 3 minutes. Add noodles; toss lightly.

SAUCES AND SIDE DISHES

■ GARDEN GLORY VEGETABLES

4 to 6 servings

1½ cups diagonally-cut carrot
    slices
1 cup diagonally-cut celery
    slices
1 tablespoon PARKAY
    Margarine
1 cup pea pods
½ cup walnut halves
    Dash of pepper
½ lb. VELVEETA Pasteurized
    Process Cheese Spread,
    cubed
2 tablespoons milk

Saute carrots and celery in margarine until crisp-tender. Reduce heat to low. Add pea pods, walnuts and pepper; mix lightly. Add process cheese spread and milk; stir until process cheese spread is melted.

Preparation time: 15 minutes
Cooking time: 15 minutes

Microwave: Reduce milk to 1 tablespoon. Combine carrots, celery and margarine in 1½-quart microwave-safe bowl. Cover with plastic wrap; vent. Microwave on High 4 to 6 minutes or until vegetables are crisp-tender. Stir in remaining ingredients. Microwave on High 2 to 3 minutes or until process cheese spread is melted, stirring after 2 minutes.

Garden Glory Vegetables

■ CARROT-PEPPER POTPOURRI

4 servings

1½ cups diagonally-cut carrot
     slices
  1 tablespoon PARKAY
     Margarine
  1 medium green pepper, cut
     into strips
  ¼ lb. VELVEETA Pasteurized
     Process Cheese Spread,
     cubed
  2 tablespoons milk
  2 tablespoons sliced almonds,
     toasted

In large skillet, stir-fry carrots in margarine 3 minutes. Add peppers; stir-fry until vegetables are crisp-tender. Reduce heat to low. Add process cheese spread and milk; stir until process cheese spread is melted. Top with almonds.

Preparation time: 5 minutes
Cooking time: 10 minutes

Microwave: Decrease milk to 1 tablespoon. Microwave carrots and margarine in 1-quart microwave-safe bowl on High 4 to 6 minutes or until crisp-tender, stirring every 2 minutes. Stir in peppers; microwave on High 2 minutes. Stir in process cheese spread and milk. Microwave on High 1 to 2 minutes or until process cheese spread is melted; mix well. Top with almonds.

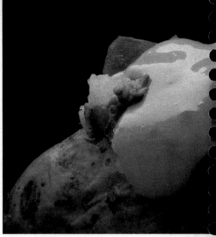

Hot 'n Spicy Potatoes

■ HOT 'N SPICY POTATOES

4 servings

  2 cups chopped broccoli
  1 tablespoon PARKAY
     Margarine
  ½ lb. VELVEETA Mexican
     Pasteurized Process Cheese
     Spread with Jalapeño
     Pepper, cubed
  2 tablespoons milk
  4 hot baked potatoes, partially
     split
  ½ cup chopped tomato

Saute broccoli in margarine 5 to 7 minutes or until crisp-tender. Combine process cheese spread and milk in saucepan; stir over low heat until

process cheese spread is melted. Top potatoes with broccoli, tomatoes and process cheese spread mixture.

Preparation time: 60 minutes
Cooking time: 15 minutes

Microwave: Microwave broccoli and margarine in 1½-quart microwave-safe bowl on High 3 to 4 minutes or until crisp-tender, stirring after 3 minutes. Microwave process cheese spread and milk in 1-quart microwave-safe bowl on High 2 to 3 minutes or until process cheese spread is melted. Top potatoes with broccoli, tomatoes and process cheese spread mixture.

■ SUNNY FRIES

4 servings

> 1 14-oz. pkg. frozen cottage fries french fried potatoes
> ¼ lb. VELVEETA Pasteurized Process Cheese Spread, cubed
> 2 tablespoons milk
> ½ teaspoon dry mustard

Prepare potatoes as directed on package. Combine process cheese spread, milk and mustard in saucepan; stir over low heat until process cheese spread is melted. Serve over hot cooked potatoes.

Preparation time: 5 minutes
Cooking time: 15 minutes

Microwave: Prepare potatoes as directed on package. Microwave process cheese spread, milk and mustard in 1-quart microwave-safe bowl on High 2½ to 3½ minutes or until process cheese spread is melted, stirring every minute. Serve over hot cooked potatoes.

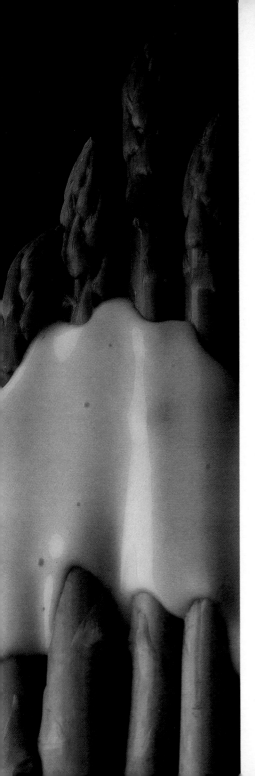

■ "VELVEETA" SAUCE

1 cup

> ½ **lb. VELVEETA Pasteurized Process Cheese Spread, cubed**
> ¼ **cup milk**

Combine ingredients in saucepan; stir over low heat until process cheese spread is melted. Serve over hot cooked pasta, vegetables or fish.

Preparation time: 5 minutes
Cooking time: 10 minutes

Variations: Add 2½-oz. jar sliced mushrooms, drained, chopped.

Add 4 crisply cooked bacon slices, crumbled.

Microwave: Combine ingredients in 1½-quart microwave-safe bowl. Microwave on High 2½ to 4½ minutes or until process cheese spread is melted, stirring every minute. Serve over hot cooked pasta, vegetables or fish.

■ CAULIFLOWER CROWN

4 to 6 servings

> ½ **lb. VELVEETA Pasteurized Process Cheese Spread, cubed**
> 2 **tablespoons milk**
> 1 **teaspoon KRAFT Pure Prepared Mustard**
> 1 **head cauliflower, cooked**
> ½ **cup diagonally-cut carrot slices, cooked**
> ½ **cup cut green beans, cooked**

"Velveeta" Sauce

Combine process cheese spread, milk and mustard in saucepan; stir over low heat until process cheese spread is melted. Remove flowerets from center of cauliflower, leaving outer ring intact. Place cauliflower ring on serving plate; surround with flowerets. Fill center of cauliflower with carrots and beans; top with process cheese spread mixture.

Preparation time: 15 minutes
Cooking time: 10 minutes

Microwave: Microwave process cheese spread, milk and mustard in 1-quart microwave-safe bowl on High 2½ to 4½ minutes or until process cheese spread is melted, stirring every minute. Continue as directed.

■ QUICK POTATO TOPPER

4 servings

½ lb. VELVEETA Pasteurized
    Process Cheese Spread,
    cubed
¼ cup milk
3 crisply cooked bacon slices,
    crumbled
4 hot baked potatoes, partially
    split
Green onion slices

Combine process cheese spread and milk in saucepan; stir over low heat until process cheese spread is melted. Stir in bacon. Serve process cheese spread mixture over potatoes. Top with onions.

Preparation time: 60 minutes
Cooking time: 10 minutes

Microwave: Microwave process cheese spread and milk in 1½-quart microwave-safe bowl on High 2½ to 4½ minutes or until process cheese spread is melted, stirring every minute. Stir in bacon. Serve process cheese spread mixture over potatoes. Top with onions.

■ CORN POLENTA

6 servings

3 cups cold water
1 cup yellow cornmeal
1 10-oz. pkg. frozen corn,
    cooked, drained
½ lb. VELVEETA Pasteurized
    Process Cheese Spread,
    cubed

In 2-quart saucepan, heat water until boiling. Gradually add cornmeal, stirring constantly. Reduce heat; cook, stirring constantly, until thickened. Add corn and process cheese spread; stir until process cheese spread is melted.

Preparation time: 5 minutes
Cooking time: 15 minutes

Microwave: Microwave water in 2-quart microwave-safe bowl on High 7 to 9 minutes or until boiling. Gradually add cornmeal; mix well. Microwave on High 2 minutes, stirring after 1 minute. Add corn and process cheese spread. Microwave on High 1 minute or until process cheese spread is melted. Stir.

■ GOLDEN GREEN BEANS

4 to 6 servings

> 2 9-oz. pkgs. frozen cut green
>   beans
> ½ lb. VELVEETA Pasteurized
>   Process Cheese Spread,
>   cubed
> 6 crisply cooked bacon slices,
>   crumbled
> 1 tablespoon finely chopped
>   onion

Cook green beans as directed on package; drain. In large bowl, combine ingredients; mix lightly. Spoon into 1-quart casserole. Bake at 350°, 15 minutes.

Preparation time: 20 minutes
Baking time: 15 minutes

Microwave: Microwave green beans as directed on package; drain. Combine ingredients in 1½-quart microwave-safe bowl; mix lightly. Microwave on High 5 to 6 minutes or until process cheese spread is melted, stirring every 2 minutes. Let stand 2 minutes.

■ TWICE-BAKED CHEESY POTATOES

8 servings

> 4 hot baked potatoes
> 2 tablespoons PARKAY
>   Margarine
> 1 tablespoon milk
> ¼ lb. VELVEETA Pasteurized
>   Process Cheese Spread,
>   cubed
> 4 crisply cooked bacon slices,
>   crumbled
> 1 tablespoon chopped fresh
>   chives

Cut potatoes in half lengthwise; scoop out centers, leaving ⅛-inch shell. Mash potatoes. Add margarine and milk; beat until fluffy. Reserve ¼ cup process cheese spread and 1 tablespoon bacon. Add chives, remaining process cheese spread and bacon to potatoes; mix lightly. Spoon into shells. Bake at 350°, 10 minutes. Top with reserved process cheese spread and bacon. Continue baking until process cheese spread begins to melt.

Preparation time: 70 minutes
Baking time: 15 minutes

Microwave: Assemble potatoes as directed. Place on microwave-safe plate. Microwave on High 3 to 4 minutes, turning plate after 2 minutes. Top with reserved process cheese spread and bacon. Microwave on High 30 seconds to 1 minute, or until process cheese spread begins to melt.

Peppy Peppers

■ PEPPY PEPPERS

6 servings

3 red, yellow or green peppers,
  cut in half lengthwise
1 4.5-oz. pkg. Spanish rice,
  cooked
¼ lb. VELVEETA Mexican
  Pasteurized Process Cheese
  Spread with Jalapeño
  Pepper, cubed
¼ cup celery slices
1 tablespoon chopped cilantro

Remove seeds from peppers. Combine remaining ingredients; mix
lightly. Fill each pepper with approximately ⅓ cup rice mixture;
place in shallow baking dish. Cover.
Bake at 350°, 30 to 35 minutes or
until thoroughly heated.

Preparation time: 15 minutes
Baking time: 35 minutes

Variation: Substitute parsley for
cilantro.

Microwave: Remove seeds from peppers. Prepare rice mixture as directed. Fill each pepper with approximately ⅓ cup rice mixture; place in
shallow microwave-safe dish. Cover
with plastic wrap; vent. Microwave
on High 5 minutes. Rearrange peppers. Cover; microwave on High 2
to 4 minutes or until thoroughly
heated.

RAINBOW VEGETABLE MEDLEY

4 servings

1 cup broccoli floweretes
1 cup yellow squash slices
½ cup peeled jicama slices cut into quarters
½ cup red pepper cut into 2-inch strips
2 tablespoons PARKAY Margarine
¼ lb. VELVEETA Pasteurized Process Cheese Spread, cubed
1 tablespoon milk
1 teaspoon rice wine
¼ teaspoon sesame oil

In large skillet, stir-fry vegetables in margarine until crisp-tender. Reduce heat to low. Stir in remaining ingredients; cook until process cheese spread is melted.

Preparation time: 10 minutes
Cooking time: 10 minutes

Variation: Omit rice wine and sesame oil.

Microwave: Microwave vegetables in margarine in 2-quart microwave-safe casserole on High 4 to 6 minutes or until crisp-tender, stirring every 2 minutes. Stir in remaining ingredients; microwave on High 2 minutes or until process cheese spread is melted. Mix well.

PRONTO ZUCCHINI

4 to 6 servings

4 cups mushroom slices
4 cups zucchini slices
¼ cup PARKAY Margarine
½ cup spaghetti sauce
¼ lb. VELVEETA Pasteurized Process Cheese Spread, cubed
2 teaspoons dried oregano leaves, crushed

In large skillet, saute vegetables in margarine until crisp-tender. Drain. Reduce heat to low. Add sauce, process cheese spread and oregano; stir until process cheese spread is melted.

Preparation time: 10 minutes
Cooking time: 15 minutes

Variation: Substitute 2 tablespoons chopped fresh oregano leaves for dried oregano leaves.

CABBAGE STIR-FRY

6 servings

4 cups chopped cabbage
1 cup thin carrot sticks
1 cup chopped onion
¼ cup PARKAY Margarine
1 6-oz. pkg. frozen pea pods, partially thawed, drained
½ lb. VELVEETA Pasteurized Process Cheese Spread, cubed

In large skillet, stir-fry cabbage, carrots and onions in margarine until crisp-tender. Reduce heat to low. Add remaining ingredients; stir until process cheese spread is melted. Serve over chow mein noodles or hot cooked rice.

Preparation time: 20 minutes
Cooking time: 10 minutes

■ POTPOURRI POTATO BOATS

4 servings

1 cup thick celery slices
1 cup green pepper strips
2 tablespoons PARKAY
  Margarine
3 tablespoons flour
1 cup milk
½ lb. VELVEETA Pasteurized
  Process Cheese Spread,
  cubed
1 4-oz. can mushrooms, drained
2 tablespoons chopped pimento
4 hot baked potatoes, partially
  split

In large skillet, saute celery and peppers in margarine. Reduce heat to low. Blend in flour. Gradually add milk; cook, stirring constantly, until thickened. Add process cheese spread, mushrooms and pimento; stir until process cheese spread is melted. Serve over potatoes.

Preparation time: 60 minutes
Cooking time: 15 minutes

■ SPICY BEAN TOSS

4 to 6 servings

1 9-oz. pkg. frozen Italian green
  beans, thawed, drained
1 cup red or green pepper strips
1 medium onion, sliced
3 tablespoons PARKAY
  Margarine
1 8¾-oz. can garbanzo beans,
  drained
⅓ cup pitted ripe olive slices
¾ teaspoon Italian seasoning
½ lb. VELVEETA Pasteurized
  Process Cheese Spread,
  cubed
¼ cup milk

In large skillet, stir-fry Italian beans, peppers and onions in margarine until crisp-tender. Add garbanzo beans, olives and Italian seasoning; mix lightly. Reduce heat to low. Add process cheese spread and milk; stir until process cheese spread is melted.

Preparation time: 15 minutes
Cooking time: 15 minutes

■ GOLDEN CORN CASSEROLE

8 servings

½ lb. VELVEETA Pasteurized
  Process Cheese Spread,
  cubed
½ cup milk
1 12-oz. can whole kernel corn,
  drained
2 eggs, beaten
¼ cup chopped green pepper
½ teaspoon dried basil leaves,
  crushed
⅛ teaspoon pepper

Combine process cheese spread and milk in saucepan; stir over low heat until smooth. Add remaining ingredients; mix well. Pour into 10×6-inch baking dish. Bake at 350°, 30 minutes or until set.

Preparation time: 10 minutes
Baking time: 30 minutes

GERMAN POTATO BAKE

6 servings

4 cups cubed hot cooked
   potatoes
½ lb. VELVEETA Pasteurized
   Process Cheese Spread,
   cubed
2 tablespoons PARKAY
   Margarine
5 crisply cooked bacon slices,
   crumbled
¼ cup green onion slices
¾ cup MIRACLE WHIP Salad
   Dressing
¼ cup sour cream
1 2-oz. jar chopped pimento,
   drained
¼ teaspoon pepper
¼ teaspoon paprika

In large saucepan, combine potatoes, ¼ lb. process cheese spread and margarine; stir over low heat until process cheese spread is melted. Add 2 tablespoons bacon, 2 tablespoons onions, salad dressing, sour cream, pimento and pepper; mix well. Spoon into 1½-quart casserole. Top with remaining process cheese spread, bacon and onions. Sprinkle with paprika. Bake at 350°, 20 to 25 minutes or until thoroughly heated.

Preparation time: 30 minutes
Baking time: 25 minutes

Variation: Substitute ¼ cup chopped red pepper for pimento.

VEGETABLE GOLDEN SAUCE

1 cup

2 tablespoons finely chopped
   celery
2 tablespoons finely chopped
   onion
1 tablespoon PARKAY
   Margarine
½ lb. VELVEETA Pasteurized
   Process Cheese Spread,
   cubed
¼ cup milk

In large skillet, saute celery and onions in margarine. Reduce heat to low. Add process cheese spread and milk; stir until process cheese spread is melted. Serve over hot cooked cauliflower or broccoli.

Preparation time: 5 minutes
Cooking time: 10 minutes

Variations: Substitute green pepper for celery.

Add 2 tablespoons chopped red pepper.

Microwave: Microwave celery, onions and margarine in 1½-quart microwave-safe bowl on High 1 to 1½ minutes or until vegetables are tender. Add process cheese spread and milk. Microwave on High 2½ to 4½ minutes or until process cheese spread is melted, stirring every minute. Serve over hot cooked cauliflower or broccoli.

German Potato Bake

■ VEGETABLE SCALLOP

6 to 8 servings

>   6 cups chopped cabbage
>   2 cups thin carrot slices
>   2 tablespoons flour
>   ½ lb. VELVEETA Pasteurized
>   Process Cheese Spread,
>   cubed
>   ¼ cup milk
>   1 teaspoon KRAFT Pure
>   Prepared Mustard
>   Dash of ground red pepper
>   1 cup fresh bread crumbs
>   2 tablespoons PARKAY
>   Margarine, melted

Combine vegetables and flour. Spoon into 12×8-inch baking dish. Combine process cheese spread, milk, mustard and red pepper in saucepan; stir over low heat until process cheese spread is melted. Pour over vegetable mixture; top with combined crumbs and margarine. Bake at 350°, 50 to 55 minutes or until vegetables are tender.

Preparation time: 20 minutes
Baking time: 55 minutes

Microwave: Omit crumbs and margarine. Combine vegetables and flour. Combine process cheese spread, milk, mustard and red pepper in 3-quart microwave-safe bowl. Microwave on High 2 to 3 minutes or until process cheese spread is melted, stirring after 2 minutes. Stir in vegetable mixture. Cover with plastic wrap; vent. Microwave on High 10 to 15 minutes or until vegetables are tender, stirring after 10 minutes. Let stand covered 2 minutes.

■ EASY "HOLLANDAISE" SAUCE

1¼ cups

>   ½ lb. VELVEETA Pasteurized
>   Process Cheese Spread,
>   cubed
>   ¼ cup milk
>   ¼ teaspoon paprika
>   1 egg, beaten
>   2 teaspoons lemon juice

Combine process cheese spread, milk and paprika in saucepan; stir over low heat until process cheese spread is melted. Stir small amount of hot mixture into egg; return to hot mixture. Cook, stirring constantly, over low heat until thickened. Stir in juice. Serve over hot cooked vegetables or fish.

Preparation time: 5 minutes
Cooking time: 15 minutes

Microwave: Microwave process cheese spread, milk and paprika in 1-quart microwave-safe bowl. Microwave on High 2½ to 3½ minutes or until process cheese spread is melted, stirring every minute. Stir small amount of hot mixture into egg; return to hot mixture. Microwave on Medium (50%) 1 to 1½ minutes or until thickened, stirring every 30 seconds. Stir in juice. Serve over hot cooked vegetables or fish.

Spinach Squares

■ SPINACH SQUARES

8 to 10 servings

  1 10-oz. pkg. frozen chopped
     spinach, cooked, well-
     drained
  ⅓ cup chopped onion
  ⅓ cup chopped red pepper
  ½ lb. VELVEETA Pasteurized
     Process Cheese Spread,
     cubed
  2 cups cooked rice
  3 eggs, beaten
  ⅛ teaspoon pepper

In large bowl, combine ingredients;
spoon into greased 10×6-inch baking
dish. Bake at 350°, 25 minutes. Let
stand 5 minutes before serving. Cut
into squares.

Preparation time: 10 minutes
Baking time: 25 minutes plus
*   standing*

■ BROCCOLI CASSEROLE

6 to 8 servings

  2 10-oz. pkgs. frozen chopped
     broccoli, thawed, drained
1½ cups cooked rice
  1 10¾-oz. can condensed cream
     of mushroom soup
  ¾ lb. VELVEETA Pasteurized
     Process Cheese Spread,
     cubed
  1 2.8-oz. can French fried
     onions

In large bowl, combine broccoli, rice,
soup, process cheese spread and 1
cup onions; mix well. Spoon into 1½-
quart casserole. Bake at 350°, 35
minutes. Top with remaining onions;
continue baking 5 minutes.

Preparation time: 10 minutes
Baking time: 40 minutes

Tex-Mex Vegetable Mix

■ TEX-MEX VEGETABLE MIX

4 to 6 servings

1 9-oz. pkg. frozen cut green
  beans, thawed, drained
1 medium red or green pepper,
  cut into strips
1 medium onion, sliced
3 tablespoons PARKAY
  Margarine
1 8¾-oz. can whole kernel corn,
  drained
½ lb. VELVEETA Mexican
  Pasteurized Process Cheese
  Spread with Jalapeño
  Pepper, cubed
2 tablespoons milk
⅓ cup slivered almonds, toasted

In large skillet, saute beans, peppers
and onions in margarine until crisp-
tender. Add corn; mix lightly. Reduce heat to low. Add process cheese
spread and milk; stir until process
cheese spread is melted. Top with
almonds just before serving.

Preparation time: 15 minutes
Cooking time: 10 minutes

Variation: Substitute VELVEETA Pas-
teurized Process Cheese Spread for
Process Cheese Spread with Jalapeño
Pepper.

Microwave: Reduce milk to 1 tablespoon. Microwave beans, peppers,
onions and margarine in 2-quart
microwave-safe bowl on High 2 to 4
minutes or until crisp-tender, stirring
after 2 minutes. Stir in corn, process
cheese spread and milk; microwave
on High 2 to 4 minutes or until process cheese spread is melted, stirring
after 2 minutes. Top with almonds
just before serving.

SOUTHWEST POTATO PUFFS

4 servings

4 medium hot baked potatoes
1 tablespoon PARKAY Margarine
1 tablespoon milk
¼ teaspoon salt
¼ lb. VELVEETA Mexican Pasteurized Process Cheese Spread with Jalapeño Pepper, cubed

Slice tops from potatoes; scoop out centers, leaving ⅛-inch shell. Mash potatoes. Add margarine, milk and salt; beat until fluffy. Stir in process cheese spread; spoon into shells. Bake at 375°, 20 minutes.

Preparation time: 70 minutes
Baking time: 20 minutes

Microwave: Assemble potatoes as directed. Place on microwave-safe plate. Microwave on High 2 to 4 minutes or until thoroughly heated, rearranging after 2 minutes.

DILL SAUCE SUPREME

1½ cups

½ lb. VELVEETA Pasteurized Process Cheese Spread, cubed
½ cup KRAFT Real Mayonnaise
¼ cup milk
¼ teaspoon dill weed

Combine process cheese spread, mayonnaise and milk in saucepan; stir over low heat until process cheese spread is melted. Stir in dill. Serve over hot cooked fish or vegetables.

Preparation time: 5 minutes
Cooking time: 10 minutes

Variations: Substitute ½ teaspoon dry mustard for dill weed.

Substitute 2 teaspoons KRAFT Prepared Horseradish for dill weed.

Microwave: Combine ingredients in 1-quart microwave-safe bowl. Microwave on High 3 to 5 minutes or until process cheese spread is melted, stirring every minute. Serve over hot cooked fish or vegetables.

GOLDEN MASHED POTATOES

4 to 6 servings

2½ cups cubed cooked potatoes, mashed
3 tablespoons milk
2 tablespoons PARKAY Margarine
1 tablespoon chopped fresh chives
½ lb. VELVEETA Pasteurized Process Cheese Spread, cubed
¼ cup (1 oz.) KRAFT 100% Grated Parmesan Cheese

Combine potatoes, milk, margarine and chives; beat until fluffy. Stir in half of process cheese spread. Spoon into 1-quart casserole; sprinkle with parmesan cheese. Bake at 350°, 20 to 25 minutes or until thoroughly heated. Top with remaining process cheese spread; continue baking until process cheese spread begins to melt.

Preparation time: 20 minutes
Baking time: 30 minutes

SOUPS AND SALADS

■ PATIO CHICKEN SALAD

6 servings

> ½ lb. VELVEETA Pasteurized
>   Process Cheese Spread,
>   cubed
> 2 cups cubed cooked chicken
> 1 8¼-oz. can pineapple chunks,
>   drained
> 1 cup celery slices
> 1 cup red or green grape halves
>   MIRACLE WHIP Salad Dressing

In large bowl, combine process cheese spread, chicken, pineapple, celery, grapes and enough salad dressing to moisten; mix lightly. Serve on lettuce-covered plates.

Preparation time: 20 minutes

Variations: Add ⅓ cup sliced almonds, toasted.

Substitute two 6½-oz. cans tuna, drained, flaked, for chicken.

Patio Chicken Salad

Vegetable-Cheese Soup

■ VEGETABLE-CHEESE SOUP

Six 1-cup servings

2 cups cubed potatoes
1½ cups cold water
1 cup carrot slices
⅓ cup chopped onion
Dash of pepper
1 lb. VELVEETA Pasteurized Process Cheese Spread, cubed
1 9-oz. pkg. frozen cut green beans, thawed, drained
½ cup beer
1 teaspoon dried marjoram leaves, crushed

In large saucepan, combine potatoes, water, carrots, onions and pepper; bring to boil. Cover; simmer 30 minutes or until vegetables are tender. Stir in remaining ingredients; continue heating until process cheese spread is melted.

Preparation time: 15 minutes
Cooking time: 40 minutes

Variation: Substitute milk for beer.

Microwave: Decrease water to 1 cup. In 2-quart microwave-safe bowl, combine potatoes, water, carrots, onions and pepper. Cover with plastic wrap; vent. Microwave on High 12 to 16 minutes or until vegetables are tender, stirring every 4 minutes. Stir in remaining ingredients; microwave on High 4 to 6 minutes or until process cheese spread is melted, stirring every 2 minutes.

■ TEXICALI SALAD

6 servings

½ **lb. ground beef**
1 **8-oz. can kidney beans, undrained**
1 **qt. shredded lettuce**
1 **cup (4 ozs.) VELVEETA Mexican Shredded Pasteurized Process Cheese Food with Jalapeño Pepper**
1 **cup chopped peeled avocado**
1 **cup chopped tomato**
¼ **cup green onion slices**
½ **cup CATALINA French Dressing**
3½ **cups (4 ozs.) tortilla chips, broken**

Brown meat; drain. Stir in beans; simmer 10 minutes. In large bowl, combine meat mixture, lettuce, process cheese food, avocados, tomatoes and onions; toss lightly. Add dressing and chips; mix lightly. Serve immediately.

Preparation time: 25 minutes
Cooking time: 15 minutes

Microwave: Crumble meat into 1-quart microwave-safe bowl. Microwave on High 3 to 5 minutes, stirring after 3 minutes; drain. Stir in beans. Microwave on High 2 to 4 minutes or until thoroughly heated, stirring after 2 minutes. In large bowl, combine meat mixture, lettuce, process cheese food, avocados, tomatoes and onions; toss lightly. Add dressing and chips; mix lightly. Serve immediately.

MONTEREY CHEESE SOUP

Five 1-cup servings

- 1 14½-oz. can tomatoes
- 6 6-inch corn tortillas, cut into ¼-inch strips
- Oil
- ½ cup chopped onion
- 2 garlic cloves, minced
- 1 lb. VELVEETA Pasteurized Process Cheese Spread, cubed
- 1 13¾-oz. can chicken broth
- 2 tablespoons chopped cilantro

Drain tomatoes, reserving ½ cup liquid. Chop tomatoes. Fry tortillas in large skillet in ¼-inch hot oil until crisp but not brown. Drain oil, reserving 2 tablespoons. Saute onions and garlic in reserved oil until onions are tender. Reduce heat to low. Add tomatoes, reserved liquid, process cheese spread, broth and cilantro. Stir until process cheese spread is melted. Divide tortillas among five soup bowls; top with process cheese spread mixture.

Preparation time: 10 minutes
Cooking time: 15 minutes

Variations: Substitute parsley for cilantro.

Substitute VELVEETA Mexican Pasteurized Process Cheese Spread with Jalapeño Pepper for Process Cheese Spread.

Microwave: Prepare tortillas as directed. Drain tomatoes, reserving ¼ cup liquid. Chop tomatoes. Combine onions, garlic and 1 tablespoon oil in 2½-quart microwave-safe bowl. Microwave on High 2 to 3 minutes or until onions are tender. Add tomatoes, reserved liquid, process cheese spread, broth and cilantro. Microwave on High 6 to 8 minutes or until process cheese spread is melted, stirring every 3 minutes. Divide tortillas among five soup bowls; top with process cheese spread mixture.

FIESTA BEAN SALAD

6 to 8 servings

- 1 16-oz. can kidney beans, drained
- ½ lb. VELVEETA Mexican Pasteurized Process Cheese Spread with Jalapeño Pepper, cubed
- 3 hard-cooked eggs, coarsely chopped
- 1 cup celery slices
- ½ cup onion rings
- ½ cup KRAFT Thousand Island Dressing
- 1 teaspoon salt

Combine ingredients; mix lightly. Cover and chill. Serve on lettuce-covered platter, if desired.

Preparation time: 30 minutes plus chilling

Fiesta Bean Salad

Cheesy Shrimp Bisque

■ CHEESY SHRIMP BISQUE

Five 1-cup servings

½ cup celery slices
2 tablespoons PARKAY Margarine
1 8-oz. pkg. PHILADELPHIA BRAND Cream Cheese, cubed
1 cup milk
½ lb. VELVEETA Pasteurized Process Cheese Spread, cubed
1 6-oz. bag frozen cooked tiny shrimp, thawed, drained
⅓ cup dry white wine
¼ teaspoon dill weed

In 2-quart saucepan, cook celery in margarine until tender. Reduce heat to medium. Add cream cheese and milk; stir until cream cheese is melted. Add process cheese spread, shrimp and wine; heat thoroughly, stirring occasionally. Sprinkle with dill before serving. Serve with crackers, if desired.

Preparation time: 10 minutes
Cooking time: 20 minutes

Variation: Omit wine. Increase milk to 1⅓ cups.

Microwave: Decrease milk to ½ cup and wine to ¼ cup. In 2-quart microwave-safe bowl, microwave celery and margarine on High 1 to 2 minutes or until celery is tender. Add milk; microwave on High 2 to 3 minutes, stirring after 2 minutes. Stir in cream cheese; microwave on High 4 to 6 minutes or until cream cheese is melted, stirring every 2 minutes. Stir in process cheese spread, shrimp and wine; microwave on High 2 to 3 minutes or until thoroughly heated. Sprinkle with dill before serving. Serve with crackers, if desired.

ACAPULCO LAYERED SALAD

6 servings

½ cup MIRACLE WHIP Salad
   Dressing
½ cup CATALINA French
   Dressing
2 cups (8 ozs.) VELVEETA
   Mexican Shredded
   Pasteurized Process Cheese
   Food with Jalapeño Pepper
1 qt. shredded lettuce
1 cup chopped green pepper
1 12-oz. can whole kernel corn
   with sweet peppers, drained
1 cup chopped zucchini
2 cups chopped tomato
1 cup celery slices
8 crisply cooked bacon slices,
   crumbled

Combine dressings; mix well. Stir in 1 cup process cheese food. In 2½-quart serving bowl, layer lettuce, peppers, corn, zucchini, tomatoes and celery. Spoon dressing mixture over salad; spread to edges of bowl to seal. Cover; chill. Sprinkle with remaining process cheese food and bacon just before serving.

Preparation time: 30 minutes plus
chilling

SPICY CORN SOUP

Four ¾-cup servings

½ cup chopped green pepper
1 tablespoon PARKAY
   Margarine
1 3-oz. pkg. PHILADELPHIA
   BRAND Cream Cheese,
   cubed
1 8¾-oz. can cream-style corn
½ lb. VELVEETA Mexican
   Pasteurized Process Cheese
   Spread with Jalapeño
   Pepper, cubed
¾ cup milk
   Corn chips

In 2-quart saucepan, saute peppers in margarine. Reduce heat to low. Add cream cheese; stir until melted. Stir in corn, process cheese spread and milk. Heat, stirring occasionally, until process cheese spread is melted and soup is thoroughly heated. Top with chips.

Preparation time: 10 minutes
Cooking time: 15 minutes

Microwave: Microwave peppers and margarine in 2-quart microwave-safe bowl on High 1 minute or until tender. Add cream cheese and milk. Cover with plastic wrap; vent. Microwave on High 2 to 3 minutes or until cream cheese is melted, stirring after 2 minutes. Stir in process cheese spread and corn. Microwave on High 4 to 5 minutes or until process cheese spread is melted, stirring every 2 minutes. Top with chips.

HEARTY AUTUMN SOUP

Five 1-cup servings

- ½ lb. bulk pork sausage
- 2 cups cold water
- 2 cups zucchini slices
- ¼ cup chopped onion
- ½ cup elbow macaroni
- ¾ lb. VELVEETA Pasteurized Process Cheese Spread, cubed

In large saucepan, brown sausage; drain. Add water, vegetables and macaroni; bring to boil. Cover; simmer 10 minutes or until macaroni is tender, stirring occasionally. Add process cheese spread; stir until process cheese spread is melted.

Preparation time: 10 minutes
Cooking time: 18 minutes

Microwave: Decrease water to 1½ cups. Crumble sausage into 2-quart microwave-safe bowl. Microwave on High 5 to 6 minutes, stirring after 3 minutes; drain. Stir in water, vegetables and macaroni. Cover with plastic wrap; vent. Microwave on High 8 to 10 minutes or until macaroni is tender, stirring every 4 minutes. Add process cheese spread; microwave on High 2 minutes or until process cheese spread is melted. Stir.

Garden Pasta Toss

GARDEN PASTA TOSS

6 to 8 servings

- 2 cups (6 ozs.) corkscrew noodles, cooked, drained
- 2 cups zucchini slices, halved
- ½ cup chopped red pepper
- 8 crisply cooked bacon slices, crumbled
- 3 hard-cooked eggs, coarsely chopped
- 1 teaspoon dried oregano leaves, crushed
- ½ teaspoon onion powder
- ½ teaspoon pepper

* * *

- ¾ lb. VELVEETA Pasteurized Process Cheese Spread, cubed
- ¾ cup KRAFT Real Mayonnaise
- 3 tablespoons milk
- 2 teaspoons KRAFT Pure Prepared Mustard

In large bowl, combine noodles, zucchini, peppers, bacon, eggs and seasonings; mix lightly.

Combine process cheese spread, mayonnaise, milk and mustard in saucepan; stir over low heat until process cheese spread is melted. Add to macaroni mixture; mix lightly. Cover; chill. Mix lightly just before serving. Serve on lettuce-covered platter, if desired.

Preparation time: 25 minutes
Cooking time: 10 minutes plus
chilling

■ CREAMY POTATO SALAD

4 to 6 servings

4 cups cooked potato slices
2 cups (8 ozs.) VELVEETA Shredded Pasteurized Process Cheese Food
½ cup MIRACLE WHIP Salad Dressing
⅓ cup chopped celery
¼ cup KRAFT "Zesty" Italian Dressing
¼ cup green onion slices
⅛ teaspoon pepper

Combine ingredients; mix lightly. Cover; chill.

Preparation time: 30 minutes plus
chilling

■ CREAMY BROCCOLI SOUP

Five 1-cup servings

¼ cup chopped onion
1 tablespoon PARKAY Margarine
2 cups milk
1 8-oz. pkg. PHILADELPHIA BRAND Cream Cheese, cubed
¾ lb. VELVEETA Pasteurized Process Cheese Spread, cubed
1 10-oz. pkg. frozen chopped broccoli, cooked, drained
¼ teaspoon ground nutmeg
Dash of pepper

In 2-quart saucepan, saute onions in margarine until tender. Reduce heat to medium. Add milk and cream cheese; stir until cream cheese is melted. Add remaining ingredients; heat thoroughly, stirring occasionally.

Preparation time: 15 minutes
Cooking time: 15 minutes

Variations: Substitute frozen chopped spinach for broccoli.

Substitute frozen cauliflower, chopped, for broccoli.

Substitute frozen asparagus spears, chopped, for broccoli.

Microwave: Microwave onions and margarine in 2-quart microwave-safe bowl on High 30 seconds or until onions are tender. Add milk; microwave on High 4 minutes, stirring after 2 minutes. Stir in cream cheese; microwave 4 to 6 minutes or until cream cheese is melted, stirring every 2 minutes. Stir in remaining ingredients; microwave on High 30 seconds or until thoroughly heated.

■ HEARTY CHICKEN 'N RICE SOUP

Five 1-cup servings

1 13¾-oz. can chicken broth
2 cups cold water
½ cup uncooked rice
½ cup celery slices
½ cup carrot slices
¾ lb. VELVEETA Pasteurized Process Cheese Spread, cubed
1½ cups chopped cooked chicken or turkey
1 4-oz. can mushrooms, drained

In large saucepan, combine broth, water, rice, celery and carrots; bring to boil. Cover; simmer 20 to 25 minutes or until vegetables and rice are tender. Add remaining ingredients; stir until process cheese spread is melted.

Preparation time: 10 minutes
Cooking time: 30 minutes

Creamy Broccoli Soup

Summer Vegetable Combo

■ SUMMER VEGETABLE COMBO

6 to 8 servings

⅓ cup KRAFT "Zesty" Italian
  Dressing
4 cups green beans, cooked
1 cup cherry tomatoes,
  quartered
1 cup mushroom slices
1 cup (4 ozs.) VELVEETA
  Shredded Pasteurized
  Process Cheese Food

Pour dressing over combined beans
and tomatoes. Cover; marinate in re-
frigerator several hours. Just before
serving, add mushrooms and process
cheese food; toss lightly.

*Preparation time: 20 minutes plus
            marinating*

■ PRONTO SALAD

6 servings

1 qt. torn assorted greens
2 cups tomato wedges
1 cup cucumber slices
½ cup red onion rings
1½ cups (6 ozs.) VELVEETA
  Shredded Pasteurized
  Process Cheese Food
  KRAFT "Zesty" Italian
  Dressing

Arrange greens on salad plates. Top
with remaining ingredients except
dressing. Serve with dressing.

Preparation time: 10 minutes

■ ITALIAN HARVEST SOUP

Six 1-cup servings

1½ cups summer squash slices, halved
1½ cups zucchini slices, halved
1 cup shredded cabbage
½ cup shredded carrot
½ cup celery slices
½ cup chopped onion
1 garlic clove, minced
2 tablespoons oil
1 13¾-oz. can chicken broth
1 lb. VELVEETA Pasteurized Process Cheese Spread, cubed
1 teaspoon dried basil leaves, crushed
¼ teaspoon pepper

In 5-quart Dutch oven, saute vegetables and garlic in oil. Reduce heat to low. Add remaining ingredients; stir until process cheese spread is melted and soup is thoroughly heated.

Preparation time: 30 minutes
Cooking time: 15 minutes

Microwave: In 4-quart microwave-safe bowl, combine vegetables, garlic and oil. Microwave on High 2 to 4 minutes or until onions are tender. Add remaining ingredients. Cover with plastic wrap; vent. Microwave on High 11 to 13 minutes or until vegetables are tender, stirring every 6 minutes.

SANDWICHES

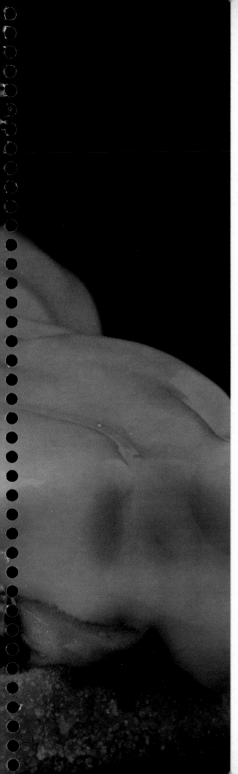

■ MUFFIN DIVAN

6 sandwiches

> 2 cups chopped cooked chicken
> 1 cup mushroom slices
> ⅓ cup picante sauce
> ¼ cup MIRACLE WHIP Salad Dressing
> 2 tablespoons green onion slices
> 3 English muffins, split, toasted
> 1 cup chopped cooked broccoli
> ½ lb. VELVEETA Pasteurized Process Cheese Spread, sliced

Combine chicken, mushrooms, sauce, salad dressing and onions; mix lightly. Top muffin halves with chicken mixture and broccoli. Place on ungreased cookie sheet. Bake at 350°, 10 minutes. Top with process cheese spread; continue baking until process cheese spread begins to melt.

Preparation time: 20 minutes
Baking time: 15 minutes

Muffin Divan

■ TEMPTING TUNA BURGERS

8 sandwiches

2 6½-oz. cans tuna, drained, flaked
1 cup dry bread crumbs
    KRAFT Thousand Island Dressing
½ cup chopped celery
2 tablespoons chopped parsley
⅛ teaspoon salt
⅛ teaspoon pepper
¾ lb. VELVEETA Pasteurized Process Cheese Spread, sliced
8 hamburger buns, split, toasted
2 cups shredded lettuce
1 2.8-oz. can French fried onions

Combine tuna, ½ cup crumbs, ⅔ cup dressing, celery, parsley and seasonings; mix lightly. Shape into eight patties. Coat with remaining crumbs. Broil on each side until lightly browned. Top each patty with process cheese spread; broil until process cheese spread begins to melt. Spread bottom halves of buns with dressing; fill buns with lettuce, patties and onions.

Preparation time: 20 minutes
Cooking time: 15 minutes

■ COUNTRY HAM SALADWICH

4 sandwiches

½ cup chopped ham
½ cup chopped celery
¼ cup chopped cucumber
¼ cup KRAFT Real Mayonnaise
2 tablespoons chopped onion
4 whole-wheat bread slices, toasted
4 tomato slices
¼ lb. VELVEETA Pasteurized Process Cheese Spread, sliced

Combine ham, celery, cucumbers, mayonnaise and onions; mix lightly. Cover toast slices with ham mixture; top with tomatoes and process cheese spread. Broil until process cheese spread begins to melt.

Preparation time: 15 minutes
Cooking time: 5 minutes

■ HOT DOG GRILLS

Frankfurter buns, split, toasted
KRAFT Pure Prepared Mustard
Frankfurters, grilled
VELVEETA Pasteurized Process Cheese Spread, sliced

Spread buns with mustard; fill with frankfurters and process cheese spread.

Preparation time: 10 minutes
Cooking time: 5 minutes

Old Tucson Tacos

■ OLD TUCSON TACOS

10 tacos

1 lb. ground beef
1 cup picante sauce
1 4¼-oz. can chopped ripe
   olives, drained
2 cups (8 ozs.) VELVEETA
   Shredded Mexican
   Pasteurized Process Cheese
   Food with Jalapeño Pepper
10 taco shells
2 cups shredded lettuce
1 cup chopped tomato

In large skillet, brown meat; drain. Add sauce, olives and 1 cup process cheese food; heat thoroughly, stirring occasionally. Fill shells with meat mixture; top with lettuce, tomatoes and remaining process cheese food.

Preparation time: 20 minutes
Cooking time: 10 minutes

Microwave: Crumble meat into 1½-quart microwave-safe bowl. Microwave on High 5 to 6 minutes, stirring after 3 minutes; drain. Stir in sauce, olives and 1 cup process cheese food. Microwave on High 4 to 5 minutes or until process cheese food is melted, stirring every 2 minutes. Fill shells with meat mixture; top with lettuce, tomatoes and remaining process cheese food.

Champion Cheese-Steak Sandwiches

■ CHAMPION CHEESE-STEAK SANDWICHES

6 sandwiches

½ lb. VELVEETA Pasteurized
    Process Cheese Spread,
    cubed
½ cup KRAFT Real Mayonnaise
¼ cup milk
1 teaspoon dry mustard
1 medium onion, sliced
2 tablespoons PARKAY
    Margarine
1 lb. thin roast beef slices
6 8-inch French bread rolls,
    split

Combine process cheese spread, mayonnaise, milk and mustard in saucepan; stir over low heat until process cheese spread is melted. Saute onions in margarine. Add meat; heat thoroughly, stirring occasionally. Fill rolls with meat mixture; top with process cheese spread mixture.

Preparation time: 20 minutes
Cooking time: 10 minutes

Microwave: Reduce margarine to 1 tablespoon. Combine process cheese spread, mayonnaise, milk and mustard in 1-quart microwave-safe bowl. Microwave on High 3 to 5 minutes or until process cheese spread is melted, stirring every minute. Combine onions and margarine in 2-quart microwave-safe bowl. Microwave on High 2 to 4 minutes or until tender, stirring after 2 minutes. Add meat; microwave on High 3 to 4 minutes or until thoroughly heated, stirring after 2 minutes. Fill rolls with meat mixture; top with process cheese spread mixture.

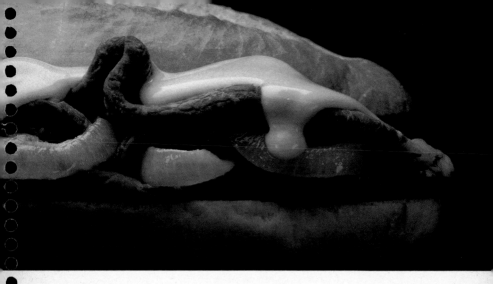

■ SLOPPY JOES

8 sandwiches

   1 lb. ground beef
   1 cup KRAFT Barbecue Sauce
   ¼ cup chopped green pepper
   ¼ cup chopped onion
   8 hamburger buns, split
   ½ lb. VELVEETA Pasteurized
      Process Cheese Spread,
      sliced

Brown meat; drain. Add barbecue sauce, peppers and onions. Cover; simmer 15 minutes, stirring occasionally. For each sandwich, cover bottom half of bun with meat mixture; top with process cheese spread. Broil until process cheese spread begins to melt. Serve with top half of bun.

Preparation time: 10 minutes
Cooking time: 30 minutes

Variation: Omit hamburger buns; substitute corn bread squares, split.

Microwave: Crumble meat into 1½-quart microwave-safe bowl; stir in peppers and onions. Microwave on High 5 to 6 minutes, stirring after 3 minutes; drain. Stir in barbecue sauce. Microwave on High 3 to 5 minutes or until thoroughly heated, stirring every 2 minutes. Continue as directed.

Cosmic Pizza

◼ COSMIC PIZZA

> **VELVEETA Pasteurized Process
> Cheese Spread, sliced
> English muffins, split, toasted
> Catsup or pizza sauce
> Frankfurters, sliced
> Sweet pickle relish**

Cut process cheese spread slices into star shapes with small cookie cutter. For each serving, spread muffin half with catsup. Top with frankfurters and relish. Broil until hot. Top with process cheese spread; continue broiling until process cheese spread begins to melt.

*Preparation time: 15 minutes
Broiling time: 10 minutes*

◼ THE "VELVEETA" GRILL

> **White bread slices
> VELVEETA Pasteurized Process
> Cheese Spread, sliced
> Soft PARKAY Margarine**

For each sandwich, top one bread slice with process cheese spread and second bread slice. Spread sandwich with margarine. Grill until lightly browned on both sides.

*Preparation time: 10 minutes
Cooking time: 5 minutes*

Variations: Substitute raisin bread slices for white bread.

Substitute rye bread slices for white bread. Top process cheese spread with tomato slice.

■ GRILLED HAM SANDWICHES

4 sandwiches

1 3-oz. pkg. PHILADELPHIA
  BRAND Cream Cheese,
  softened
2 teaspoons Dijon mustard
1 teaspoon KRAFT Prepared
  Horseradish
8 whole-wheat bread slices
½ lb. VELVEETA Pasteurized
  Process Cheese Spread,
  sliced
½ lb. boiled ham slices
  Soft PARKAY Margarine

Combine cream cheese, mustard and horseradish, mixing until well blended. For each sandwich, top one bread slice with cream cheese mixture, process cheese spread, ham and second bread slice. Spread sandwich with margarine. Grill until lightly browned on both sides.

Preparation time: 10 minutes
Cooking time: 5 minutes

■ FISH FILLET FUN

4 sandwiches

4 hamburger buns, split
  SAUCEWORKS Tartar Sauce
4 breaded fish fillets, cooked
4 tomato slices
  VELVEETA Pasteurized Process
  Cheese Spread, sliced
  Olives
  Sweet pickle slices
  Pimento

For each sandwich, spread bun with tartar sauce. Top bottom half of bun with fish, tomato and process cheese spread. Bake at 400°, 5 minutes or until process cheese spread begins to melt. To form face, use olives for eyes, pickles for nose and pimento for mouth. Serve with top half of bun.

Preparation time: 15 minutes
Baking time: 5 minutes

Variation: Substitute 8 frozen fish sticks, cooked, for fish fillets.

■ EGGS IN A POCKET

12 sandwiches

6 hard-cooked eggs, chopped
1 cup (4 ozs.) VELVEETA
  Shredded Pasteurized
  Process Cheese Food
½ cup MIRACLE WHIP Salad
  Dressing
¼ cup chopped celery
2 tablespoons chopped pitted
  ripe olives
6 pita bread rounds, cut in half
  Lettuce
  Tomato wedges

Combine eggs, process cheese food, salad dressing, celery and olives; mix lightly. Cover; chill. Fill pita halves with lettuce, tomatoes and egg mixture.

Preparation time: 30 minutes plus
chilling

FRUIT COZIES

4 sandwiches

  1 cup finely chopped ham
  ⅓ cup raisins
  ⅓ cup flaked coconut
  ⅓ cup shredded carrot
  ¼ cup MIRACLE WHIP Salad
     Dressing
  8 whole-wheat bread slices
  ¼ lb. VELVEETA Pasteurized
     Process Cheese Spread,
     sliced
     Soft PARKAY Margarine

Combine ham, raisins, coconut, carrots and salad dressing; mix lightly. For each sandwich, top one bread slice with approximately ½ cup ham mixture, process cheese spread and second bread slice. Spread sandwich with margarine. Grill until lightly browned on both sides.

Preparation time: 10 minutes
Cooking time: 10 minutes

COWBOY POCKET SANDWICHES

4 sandwiches

  ½ lb. ground beef
  ¼ cup chopped onion
  ¼ lb. VELVEETA Pasteurized
     Process Cheese Spread,
     cubed
  1 9.5-oz. can PILLSBURY
     Refrigerated Pastry Pockets

Brown meat; drain. Add onions; cook until tender. Stir in process cheese spread; remove from heat. Prepare pastry pockets according to package directions. Place on ungreased cookie sheet. Place approximately ⅓ cup meat mixture on half of each square; fold pastry in half, enclosing filling. Press edges together with fork to seal. Cut three ½-inch slits in top of each square. Bake at 375°, 12 to 15 minutes or until golden brown.

Preparation time: 20 minutes
Baking time: 15 minutes

GOLDEN BLT

     White bread slices, toasted
     KRAFT Real Mayonnaise
     VELVEETA Pasteurized Process
        Cheese Spread, sliced
     Crisply cooked bacon slices
     Lettuce
     Tomato slices

For each sandwich, spread two bread slices with mayonnaise. Cover one bread slice with process cheese spread, bacon, lettuce, tomato and second bread slice.

Preparation time: 10 minutes

Fruit Cozies

■ CHEDDARY CHICKEN SALAD GRILLS

6 sandwiches

2 cups chopped cooked chicken
¼ lb. VELVEETA Pasteurized
    Process Cheese Spread,
    cubed
¼ cup chopped celery
¼ cup KRAFT Real Mayonnaise
12 whole-wheat bread slices
    KRAFT Strawberry Preserves
    Soft PARKAY Margarine

Combine chicken, process cheese spread, celery and mayonnaise; mix lightly. For each sandwich, spread one bread slice with preserves; cover with chicken mixture and second bread slice. Spread sandwich with margarine. Grill until lightly browned on both sides.

Preparation time: 15 minutes
Cooking time: 10 minutes

■ PERFECT PORK SANDWICHES

4 sandwiches

½ cup green pepper strips
1 medium onion, sliced
2 tablespoons PARKAY
    Margarine
1 tablespoon Dijon mustard
1 lb. thin roast pork slices
4 poppy seed buns, split
¼ lb. VELVEETA Mexican
    Pasteurized Process Cheese
    Spread with Jalapeño
    Pepper, sliced

Saute vegetables in margarine. Reduce heat to low. Stir in mustard. Add meat; mix lightly. Fill buns with meat mixture and process cheese spread; wrap in foil. Bake at 300°, 10 to 15 minutes or until thoroughly heated.

Preparation time: 10 minutes
Cooking time: 15 minutes

■ TERRIFIC TURKEY SANDWICHES

4 sandwiches

1 3-oz. pkg. PHILADELPHIA
    BRAND Cream Cheese,
    softened
2 teaspoons Dijon mustard
1 teaspoon KRAFT Prepared
    Horseradish
8 whole-wheat bread slices
½ lb. VELVEETA Pasteurized
    Process Cheese Spread,
    sliced
4 cooked turkey slices
    Soft PARKAY Margarine

Combine cream cheese, mustard and horseradish, mixing until well blended. Spread approximately 1 tablespoon cream cheese mixture onto each bread slice. For each sandwich, cover one bread slice with process cheese spread, turkey and second bread slice. Spread sandwich with margarine. Grill until lightly browned on both sides.

Preparation time: 10 minutes
Cooking time: 10 minutes

THE CALIFORNIA CLASSIC

2 sandwiches

¼ cup MIRACLE WHIP Salad
  Dressing
1 teaspoon KRAFT Pure
  Prepared Mustard
4 rye bread slices
  Alfalfa sprouts
4 cooked turkey slices
¼ lb. VELVEETA Pasteurized
  Process Cheese Spread,
  sliced
  Thin tomato slices
  Peeled avocado slices

Combine salad dressing and mustard;
mix well. Spread bread slices with
salad dressing mixture. For each
sandwich, top one bread slice with
sprouts, turkey, process cheese
spread, tomatoes, avocados and second bread slice.

Preparation time: 10 minutes

Variation: Substitute salami slices or
boiled ham slices for turkey.

The California Classic

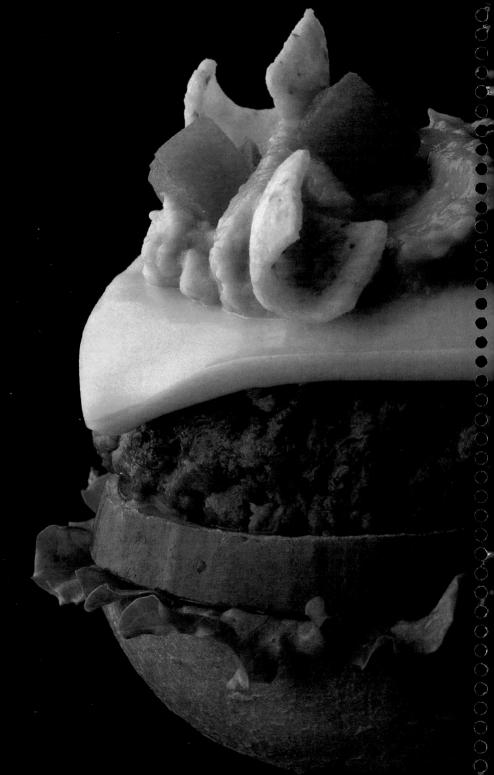

■ FIESTA BURGERS

4 sandwiches

1 lb. ground beef
⅔ cup crushed corn chips
½ cup chili sauce
¼ lb. VELVEETA Pasteurized
    Process Cheese Spread,
    sliced
4 hard rolls, split
    Lettuce
4 red onion slices
    Guacamole
    Chopped tomato

Combine meat, chips and ¼ cup chili sauce; mix lightly. Shape into four patties; place on rack of broiler pan. Broil on both sides to desired doneness. Top with process cheese spread; broil until process cheese spread begins to melt. Spread rolls with remaining chili sauce. For each sandwich, cover bottom half of roll with lettuce, onion and patty. Top with remaining ingredients, additional chips and top half of roll.

Preparation time: 10 minutes
Broiling time: 15 minutes

■ SAUSAGE BISCUITS

5 servings

1 12-oz. can BIG COUNTRY®
    Refrigerated Buttermilk
    Biscuits
10 brown 'n serve sausage patties
¼ lb. VELVEETA Pasteurized
    Process Cheese Spread,
    sliced, cut in half

Prepare biscuits and sausage patties according to package directions; split biscuits in half. For each sandwich, top biscuit half with patty, process cheese spread and second biscuit half. Bake at 400°, 3 minutes or until process cheese spread begins to melt.

Preparation time: 5 minutes
Baking time: 20 minutes

■ FRISCO BAY SANDWICHES

6 sandwiches

1 6½-oz. can tuna, drained,
    flaked
¼ lb. VELVEETA Pasteurized
    Process Cheese Spread,
    cubed
1 cup chopped apple
½ cup celery slices
    MIRACLE WHIP Salad Dressing
6 croissants, split
    Lettuce

Combine tuna, process cheese spread, apples, celery and enough salad dressing to moisten; mix lightly. Fill croissants with lettuce and tuna mixture.

Preparation time: 10 minutes

Fiesta Burgers

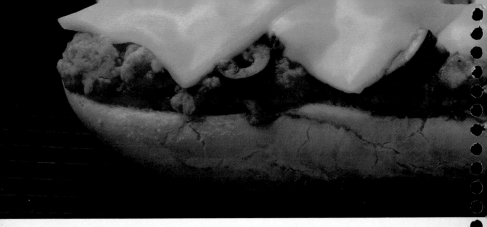

French Bread Pizza

■ FRENCH BREAD PIZZA

6 servings

½ lb. Italian sausage
1 8-oz. can pizza sauce
1 cup zucchini slices, quartered
⅓ cup pitted ripe olive slices
1 teaspoon Italian seasoning
1 14-inch French bread loaf, cut
  in half lengthwise
½ lb. VELVEETA Pasteurized
  Process Cheese Spread,
  sliced, cut in half diagonally

Remove sausage from casing. In large skillet, brown sausage; drain. Combine all ingredients except bread and process cheese spread. Place bread on ungreased cookie sheet; top both bread halves with sausage mixture. Bake at 350°, 25 to 30 minutes or until thoroughly heated. Top with process cheese spread; continue baking until process cheese spread begins to melt.

Preparation time: 15 minutes
Baking time: 35 minutes

■ SIZZLIN' APPLE MELT

4 sandwiches

2 English muffins, split, toasted
  Soft PARKAY Margarine
  KRAFT Strawberry Preserves
4 Canadian-style bacon slices
  Thin apple slices
¼ lb. VELVEETA Pasteurized
  Process Cheese Spread,
  sliced

Spread muffin halves with margarine and preserves; top with bacon and apples. Broil 3 minutes or until apples are tender. Top with process cheese spread; continue broiling until process cheese spread is melted.

Preparation time: 10 minutes
Broiling time: 5 minutes

■ GOLDEN EGG SALAD SANDWICHES

6 sandwiches

 6 hard-cooked eggs, chopped
 ¼ lb. VELVEETA Pasteurized
     Process Cheese Spread,
     cubed
 ¼ cup chopped celery
 2 tablespoons chopped green
     onion
   Dash of each salt and pepper
   KRAFT Real Mayonnaise
12 whole-wheat bread slices
   Lettuce

Combine eggs, process cheese spread, celery, onions, seasonings and enough mayonnaise to moisten; mix lightly. For each sandwich, top one bread slice with lettuce, egg mixture and second bread slice.

Preparation time: 30 minutes

■ SUB MARINER

6 sandwiches

 ½ lb. VELVEETA Pasteurized
     Process Cheese Spread,
     cubed
 ¼ cup milk
 3 6-inch French bread rolls,
     split
   Shredded cabbage
   Bologna slices
   Salami slices
   Tomato slices
   Red onion rings

Combine process cheese spread and milk in saucepan; stir over low heat until smooth. For each sandwich, cover roll half with cabbage, bologna, salami, tomatoes and onions. Top with process cheese spread mixture.

Preparation time: 10 minutes
Cooking time: 5 minutes

INDEX